Praise for *The Second Tour*

D1431990

Front cover image by Howard Sokol and Blu Hartkopp

Rootie! Rootie! Come closer Rootie.
I'm here, Benjie, I'm here, I said, clasping his hand on my arm.
Help me Rootie, my legs won't move.
Aw Benjie, it'll be okay Benj, I'll give you mine.

The Second Tour

THE SECOND TOUR

By: Terry P. Rizzuti

Spinetinglers Publishing
www.spinetinglerspublishing.com

Spinetinglers Publishing
22 Vestry Road, Co. Down BT23 6HJ, UK
www.spinetinglerspublishing.com

First edition published by Spinetinglers Publishing
11th November 2008.

Second edition published by Spinetinglers Publishing
May 2011

ISBN: 978-1-906755-21-8

Printed in the United Kingdom

DISCLAIMER

My intention in producing this work on the Vietnam War was to represent my personal experience as closely as thought possible through written form. *The Second Tour* is told as fiction because I believe fiction, specifically contemporary fiction, allows most closely the recreation of the experience of war and its effects. Since it is impossible to separate one's writing from one's experiences, it is highly likely that certain passages bear close resemblance to actual events and real people. Thus, even though there was a 2nd Battalion, 26th Marine Regiment with which I served proudly during the years 1966 and 1967, by changing names and descriptions, and by otherwise distorting facts, I hope to have universalized the experience. My greatest surprise in writing this novel was the realization that the characters came to represent not just experience but multiple facets of my own personality; their actions, in other words, were both my own and those of which I was capable. The result has been my conclusion that there were no good or bad guys in Vietnam: We Marines, at the grunt level at least, were just a bunch of boys undergoing on-the-job training under the most severe of conditions, trying to stay alive the best way we knew how in order to get home in one piece.

Terry P. Rizzuti

Portions of Part I, in slightly different form, were previously published under the title "Fragments" in the journal *War, Literature and the Arts*, edited by Donald Anderson, US Air Force Academy, English Department, Fall/Winter 1996 issue, pp. 97-102. An excerpt from Part 2 was previously published in the journal *The Christmas Cracker*, edited by John Van Peenen, The Goatfoot Press, Ponca City, OK, issue XIV, 1999, pp. 35-38.

ACKNOWLEDGMENTS

Where does one even begin to acknowledge the influences on one's work, let alone one's gratitude? In a general sense, my tendency is to reflect all the way back to childhood, to my mom who, with the words "over my dead body," usurped the job of teaching me how to read from the first-grade teacher who had given up and wanted to hold me back a year; and to my high school English teacher who brought me great happiness when he said "hey, you can write," not knowing that I had been trying very hard to do just that; and even to my college freshman English teacher who made me angry enough to walk out of class after she handed me back my first term paper with a great big C- on the front, rivers of red ink running throughout, and the comment on the last page "you write with a simplicity beyond compare," as though that in itself somehow implied mediocrity; and especially to my heroes, Balt, Benny, Bricker, Cookie, Everley, Jackson, Jeffrey, MacVey, Moffitt, Nevers, Oots, Patrick, Purvis, Rigby, Roley and all the others I can't now remember, who collectively and successfully taught me the rules of the jungle, thus increasing my chances of surviving a guerrilla war long enough to reach my 21st birthday.

But even more so, I wish to thank my daughter for her patience and understanding of my preoccupation with this novel at the expense of spending more time with her, even though she was too young then to remember now; her mother for her tolerance of my need to "get it all down before I die;" my siblings and late parents for all of their encouragement during my many years of procrastination; and Mr. and Mrs. JC Mallett for providing me the financial means to pursue graduate studies in English Literature at the University of Oklahoma.

And I thank Lela Lucy and Tom Hardy for their constructive criticism of the early drafts; and Kathy Hines for word processing the original manuscript through numerous revisions, and for her exuberance which oftentimes surpassed my own.

I am deeply, deeply indebted to Francine Stadtmiller for providing me the surprise of my life, some 95 letters I had written her from Vietnam, resource material without which this book would be vastly inferior.

And I especially thank John Drayton, senior editor at the University of Oklahoma Press; Louis Owens, an award-winning Native American fiction writer; and B. J. Robbins, a book agent, for spurring me to continue seeking publication at a time when I had seriously considered giving up.

Then there's Gerry Tate: thank you, thank you for contacting me on Authorsden.com and sending me to Jodi Dougan and Nolene Dougan at Spinetinglers.net. Jodi, thanks for your enthusiasm, guidance and Northern Irish dialect lessons; Nolene, thank you so much for the wonderful book review.

Next is my writing partner, R. E. Armstrong. His incomparable enthusiasm for writing kept me plugging away at projects through many a dark day. Thanks, Bubba; you're the best.

And I can't even begin to thank my best friend, Jin Brown. Jin stole valuable time from his doctoral studies in Communication to review, edit and discuss several early drafts through numerous stages, pointing out structural weaknesses and narration inconsistencies, and offering the kind of writing assistance and emotional support only an editor and close friend can provide.

Finally, I wish to express tremendous gratitude to my wife, Mary Banken, who, by encouraging me to visit the Vietnam Veterans Memorial in 1994, was the inspiration behind my writing of the Prologue. In a nutshell, Mary unwittingly provided me insight whereby a rather dark novel could at least point in the general direction of spiritual resolution.

To each of you I give my sincerest and most heartfelt thanks.

To my daughter Tristan,
that she might better know her father some day.

PREFACE

My first Vietnam tour lasted thirteen months and two days, but seemed a lifetime. My second tour will last forever.

TPR
April 30, 2011

In The Beginning
Is The Problem.
And Vietnam's Problem Is
Communism.

In Medias Res
Is The Solution.
And America's Solution Is
Democracy.

In The End
Is The Result. And The Result Is DEATH.

Malcolm Tent
1967

CONTENTS

PROLOGUE

I know you're up there Benjie. Hey man, it's me, Rootie. Can you believe it? Forty-seven years old with white hair, and dressed like a suit. It's your fault, you know, the white hair I mean. Sorry it took so long, but I had to wait for the right day, for when that door was open and the sun shining. You're so high I can't reach you, to touch you, so I'll just sit awhile, chat some, like we used to do. There's others up and down the line I've visited. Tommy Baker's off to your right. Smoke and George are right next to him. Stricklyn, Watson, Murphy and Wiskey are all together down the other way. But what about Nebraska, or the other guys we only knew by nickname or first name? How do I find them? Oh well, I suppose that's the breaks. Kinda wish that little girl were here too.

Panel 19E is yours, and it's a fine marker you've got here. A black shiny granite wall in a V-shaped ambush, names from the past etched into the future, facing out at all of us moving through the zone looking for signs. You didn't fool me, though. I knew you were here long before I ever saw you. The listening posts were a dead giveaway, a good diversion I must admit, what with the big gun, and especially the nurses. That threw me off some. Anyway, I circled in from the west, cautiously, to steady my nerves and size up the main body. You're dug in well, Benjie, nearly 59,000 strong; you've got us covered real good and it's not likely there'll be many survivors.

I see the reflections of others, filing behind me like shadows, pausing, watching me cry. At least it feels that way, like their eyes are on me, curiously noting my grief. I know, I know, I used to be tougher than this. Listen, it's a nice place here: beautiful, peaceful, lots of birds singing, a place of reverence, a place to reflect. I really miss you, Benjie. I think about you all the time. I think about that day twenty-seven years ago when our whole world came apart. Sometimes I wish I were up there with you; most times I'm glad I'm not.

That woman standing behind me? the patient one with the camera? She's my best friend. You'd like her a lot. Her name is Mary and she's gifted – she took this burned out shell and turned it into a lantern. I'll always love her for that. Anyway, I'm leaving you a present, wrapped in plastic to keep the rain off. It's our story and it's fiction, but I think you'll understand why once you've read it. I don't know when I'll get back here. Maybe never, maybe often. It's hard to say because I'm letting go now, moving rapidly towards closure, so take care, God bless you, and always, always remember: life's a bitch, but as long as I'm alive, you are too.

Day is done,
Gone the sun,
From the land; from the sea; from the sky.

All is well,
Rest in peace,
God is nigh; God is nigh; God is nigh.

PART 1

IN THE BEGINNING

CHAOS

We woke one morning just about light. I fired up a couple of heat tabs and started the water. Stricklyn, tossing, said he was beat. I nodded and tended the heat. Murphy sat up and yawned while the water boiled. Coffee, brewing, woke up Watson and Wiskey as the light peeped through the trees.

Noises destroyed the peace. It was always that way. Light frequently did too, but at least you could see. There's something about being able to see that makes people braver. I think that's why old people don't give a shit. Young people give a shit but they're powerless, so the anxiety from their powerlessness is exploited in the name of patriotism. God save the flag; only God is boys. Now that's power.

Stricklyn lit a joint, cupped in his palms, and passed it to me to Watson to Murphy to Wiskey who flicked it. Small fires dotted the hill. It was too light now. I moved to my rifle and sat there cradling it in my arms, my back to the others, thinking about cleaning it; and dreaming, dreaming about home and going home and being a hero coming off the plane. But life's a bitch – and then you die.

Someone behind me, I think Murphy, moved to the bushes that exploded. Watson moaned Momma over and over. I crawled away quickly, pain hurting to get out. Oh God! Oh God! I groaned and groaned. But there was no God, only blood, blood and hamburger meat. I peeked at Stricklyn, my good friend. He was dead, but he

3

was talkin' to me. God is boys, he said. Get 'em! Get 'em!

Get 'em? Hell, I couldn't even move. And I couldn't see either, and it was light.

-2-

I was born in Oklahoma, in Stillwater, in Payne County. My parents took me halfway across the country to New York to grow up. I went halfway back again to college, and then halfway around the world to war. Now that was a trip, and I never did grow up.

-3-

Call it luck, Fortune is without,
And many a nearsighted boozer drowns in milk,
To run again for their dear ol' mater alma.

Heimie told me that once. It made sense and he joined the Marine Corps, so I joined too. Now that was luck.

So I woke one morning with a leech on my dick. It felt kind of like a dull, throbbing toothache in the wrong place. I tried to piss it off but couldn't, except when I finally singed it with a lit cigarette. Fire was hot, and insect repellent burned worse than the clap. Some leeches were big like snakes. I despised them at first, but they went on loving me till I changed my attitude. Anything that could survive that climate deserved some respect, so I studied their habits long and hard, and worked a lot of overtime trying to avoid them. It gave me a sense of purpose, a reason for living.

-4-

We crossed the bridge when we came to it, but it was a whole nother ball game. Money was first, but money wasn't anything, so I went second, and second is nothing. A breeze swayed the bridge and we dropped like pointers, noses sniffing, senses wired. Money went first again but I was faster, so I'm here to tell about it. Tracers traced, flashes flashed and we lost fourteen in two hours.

4

-5-

Nebraska we called him and I liked him a lot, but he seemed short on the will to live. Three machine guns pinned us down; you'd think he'd be scared. Boys Town Champ, we called him. Could pitch a no hitter when he wanted. Grenades are like baseballs, he said. Watch this. Well he got two but they got one and our loss was greater. Call my Momma, he wanted when he died. And his brains stained my shirt sleeve as I cried inside. Nebraska talked too, rest assured of that. God is boys.

-6-

It was pouring the night Charlie hit at dusk. I was sitting on some sandbags in a bunker, writing a letter home. Lieutenant shit his pants and I could see why but it was still funny. Tiny little turds dribbled out the bottom of his trousers and followed him around like chocolate milk duds. Fire broke out in the C.O. tent and he stunk like hell, barking orders and running in circles. Claymores blew at ghosts for targets, and one outa three grenades were duds. I wonder how many leftover Vietnam grenades there'll be for the next war, I asked Surly out of genuine concern. It won't matter if it's nuclear, he answered. Everything and nothing will be leftover.

-7-

But what's wrong with me, Doc? I asked. My war experience was nearly twenty years ago. I want it to go away – although in another sense I don't ever want to forget. I just want all those people to stay dead, but they keep coming back; they keep haunting me all hours of the day and night, calling out my name like they still need my help. I can't sleep. I can't think or concentrate. It's ruining my second marriage. It's not that I'm flashbacking like in my first marriage. I'm not paranoid anymore, or thinking I'm back in Nam or anything. It's more like I re-experience the original incidents, and then live in them from the present. And I keep changing the choices I made in order to come up with different outcomes and see if my original decisions were correct.

It's called PTSD, he said. Post Traumatic Stress Disorder. I don't really know enough about it yet. It used to be called Shell Shock, and Combat Fatigue or Combat Neurosis. One thing I do know is this: you're going to have to evolve through normal grieving processes. You can't continue holding all this energy inside you. You've got to let it out, even if it means breaking down in tears.

How can I let it out, Doc? What about that little girl for Christsakes? I repressed that for nearly eighteen years. If it hadn't been for those letters I wrote, I still might not know. How many more of those little jewels are hiding out in my head? And besides, I'm afraid to grieve. I'm afraid I won't be able to stop.

And something else, Doc: Sometimes I feel like I lead two lives. In the one I'm this middle-aged man who leads a life that's construed as normal; and in the other I'm that proud, angry combat Marine who saw and did things no nineteen-year-old kid should ever experience. I'm proud because I responded to the call of the country during an historical watershed, however naively, and did my job well. And angry because the same country that trained us as killers and sent us out as food for powder blamed the outcome of the war on the grunts, the convenient scapegoats for all the bad political and military decisions made. We were used and abused, Doc. And this country hasn't learned a damn thing. It's going to happen again and again.

Reflecting on the past is a life saver in a war zone, he said quite matter-of-factly. But it's a killer in the real world. Think about this, now; it's important. Reflection is no longer going to get you through stressful situations, at least not as long as accountability to your employer and relationships with your family are important to you. My suggestion is that you take up something constructive, something creative like painting or writing.

I've started making notes to myself, I said, but they're all scrambled. There doesn't seem to be any pattern. I have to work really hard to make any sense of it because it's all a pastiche of feelings, deep feelings. I write them down as soon as I have one. I work hard at trying to understand, to find a pattern. But it's just like the original experience itself, except that there's all this emotion coming out now. And most times there didn't seem to be any sense, any order. It was pure chaos.

-8-

MAIL CALL! Man, letters were so important. I didn't exactly get a Dear John, I got a

Dear Rock,   Aug 25, 1967

I Have A Confession To Make. Remember when you came to see me just before leaving and I wouldn't let you? Well, I wouldn't let you because I was seeing other guys, but I didn't want to tell you because you were just leaving. Now I know this isn't exactly the best time to tell you, what with your asking for help and everything, but I really do love you now and please, please can you ever forgive me?

Love, Me

You see, God really is boys, but what can I say that Dylan didn't?

I'm a thinkin' and a wonderin' walkin' down the road,
I once loved a woman, a child I am told.
I gave her my heart, but she wanted my soul.
But don't think twice it's all right.

-9-

Shot a sun bear once but he died. I just wanted him to leave at first, but he kept challenging my integrity. Shot some kind of a deer too and got chewed out. Hell, every kid in upstate New York learns to shoot deer. It's almost instinctive. Shot an elephant with a LAW. It blew a hole in his side four feet square. I really felt bad about it, but hell it was pitch black and he sounded like a whole damn regiment. Shot a cobra once but kept missing. M-16s are lousy up close; the front sight's too high. The scared Vietnamese kids I was trying to help out were jumping up and down pointing at it yelling VC! VC! and I was yelling back SNAKE, GODDAMMIT, SNAKE! I got him with the fifth round, and then Raven bit him in half, just stretched that snake out real tight, chomped it in two with a big grin on his face and then spat out a hunk of raw flesh. Chunked cobra, he called it, good for the come-plexion, the die-gestion and the dispo-sition. A cobra a day keeps ya happy an' gay.

Raven was crazier than most. Saw him stab a woman in the left tit and her not even flinch. She stared him straight in the face with the kind of cold intensity that'd make yer skin crawl. I told him he'd met his match. He had tried to screw her earlier, just before she attempted cutting his balls off with a butterfly knife. He made two mistakes. The first was seeing another woman. The second was getting caught. He changed her attitude quickly though.

Shot at gooks and they shot back. Got very few that I know of for sure. I was too busy thinking up ways to stay alive. Guts was never my strong point; camouflage was. There's two things I can't stand: one is pain, the other losing, but I don't mind hiding. Insects change color, so do people some may say, but I came home to fight another way. We didn't belong there, and everyone knew it. Vietnam it was agreed was the pits; States Side, the land of the big PX, was considered the end of the rainbow.

-10-

R&R was A-okay. I went to Bangkok, a name that speaks for itself. There's a word for that. Bookoo women in Bangkok, just for the pickin' and $11 a night. Had my own cab driver too, on call twenty-four hours, only thirty bucks and a carton of smokes for five days service. Mr. Eng was his name. I called him Iggy. He called me Boss Man when he wasn't calling me Doctor Zhivago. Said I looked like Omar Sharif. I told him he was outa his tree. Whenever I'd call down for room service, though, some seductive sweet voice would answer Yessss Doctor Zhivago? Send Iggy up here, I'd say. Tell him to bring some Buddha sticks. Yessss Doctor

Zhivago, and there'd be giggling on the line. Two Aussies jumped me on a dance floor one night – Iggy busted ass. Oh, I loved that man; hope I can immortalize him. Fourteen point beer and Thai sticks instead. Spent over $800 with nothing to show for it except a grin and an appetite and a bad case of wanting to go back. Oh yes, and one very lasting remembrance of Kaiko, a gorgeous Thai chick, squattin' over a toilet, her bare feet up on the seat, her bush draining like rain-drenched jungle, her smile and flickering slant eyes firing me up like a joint through a carburetor.

I managed to stay gone from my squad seventeen days total. Got back just in time to ship out on patrol. Nothing in the area, Recon said. Bullshit, I knew. Leave your helmets and flak jackets, said Captain Kody. It's 140 degrees where we're going. I wore mine anyway. Before the next afternoon, guys I didn't even know offered me hundreds of dollars for my flak jacket. Mortars, rockets and artillery were blowin' holes all around us. Thoomp, thoomp, thoomp. Ontos 106s shattered the atmosphere in retaliation, launching fireballs tearing up their ground cover like crashing four-inch meteorites. Boom, boom, boom. I hid under my helmet, or tried to. Jeffrey was right there one second; a hole took his place the next. I was gonna visit him in St. Louis when we got back. Believe me, he spoke too as I cried PAYBACK IS A MOTHER-FUCKER! But who do you pay back? asked Raven, the people who send you here or the people you're fighting? You tell me, I said. It was a short round that got him.

-11-

My Lai was tame from what I know of it, I told my political science instructor. My Lai was everywhere, but My Lai was caught, like Watergate. My Lai was hysteria generated from fear and anger, primarily fear. When your buddies are dying and you know a way to stop it, you stop it. At one level, stopping it means killing everything that moves before it kills you. The safety rule we called it. On another level I believe stopping it means exposing the horror until the horror is conscious to everyone. Kind of like attacking the problem through the back door.

-12-

One thing we didn't do was take captives. Raven came in handy for that. Prisoners and Chieu Hois became so terrified of Raven they always tried to escape. Raven concocted some very elaborate stories for why he had to empty his .45 into some gook's back.

No shit, Rootie, that mutherfucker called my momma a faggot. Said it plain as day, and in English too. I had to shoot his raggedy ass.

Six fuckin' rounds man? I said, in the blind side?

Well, he pissed me off, Rootie, then tried haulin' ass. I didn't have no choice. You know a .45 ain't all that accurate. I had to make sure. Didn't wanna go to jail for losin' no prisoner.

You make me sick, Raven, I said to him.

Yeah, he said back, what are ya gonna do, send me to Vietnam?

Sergeant Rotan was even worse. He not only had it in for gooks, but even more so for authority. He hated officers, especially lifers and Ninety-Day-Wonders. They're pussies, he told me, because they only do six-month tours in the field, and then they rotate to the rear and become desk jockeys just about the time they learn what the fuck they're doing. He shot our Ninety-Day-Wonder Second Lieutenant one night. I didn't blame him; the Lieutenant was an ignorant asshole, but if all ignorant assholes needed shooting, Sergeant's work would never be done.

-13-

You jive ass motherfucker, George said to Smoke Terryton this, the most recent of the many times Smoke was telling us he had been starting fullback for Tulane University in 1963. Smoke wasn't his real name but Terryton was. We called him Smoke for two reasons. One was the cigarette brand. The other was because he was always blowin' smoke up peoples' butts. It be true, he'd say. If my knee no give out, I still be playin'. George was pacing all around getting madder by the minute. He couldn't stand the fact that Smoke was all the time bull-shitting and no one ever did anything about it. It never occurred to George that we did nothing

10

about it because of Smoke's entertainment value. After all, watching Smoke was a lot like watching television. If we didn't like what we saw or heard at the moment, we just tuned him out.

Smoke was genuinely deranged. He had absolutely no concept of reality, until the shit hit the fan. Then he'd be shocked back to immediate attention, to the fact that gooks were trying to kill him as well as us, and the fact that he really wasn't as invulnerable as he'd have liked everyone to believe. The problem worsened, though, as time wore on because each time he survived a fire fight, Smoke came away that much more convinced he was right.

Man, he said, jew see me out dare dodgin' dem bullets?

SAY WHAT? screamed George. The onliest thing you be dodgin's yo shadow.

No lie now, said Smoke. I be seeing dem bullets comin'. Just step outs da way an they be gone by.

I be lightin' yo black ass on fire you keeps up, said George. Then we be seeing some real smoke.

Rock Phosphate was another character. We called him Rock 'cause he looked just like Sergeant Rock, the comic strip character. Malcolm Tent tagged him with the name Phosphate 'cause he smelled so bad, but actually it was because Malcolm liked to show off his knowledge and knew a little bit about earth science. Everyone was in on the joke including Rock. It really wasn't his fault that he smelled bad. It wasn't that he did anything any different from the rest of us, didn't take fewer baths or showers or anything like that. Hell none of us got to clean up very often. The problem ran deeper than that – Rock was simply plagued with a seriously bad case of BO. All of us realized that, I think; still, no one cut him any slack. He was the talk of the whole company. When he got himself blowed away up in the DMZ by sticking his nose where it didn't belong (up in the air in the middle of a fire fight), for a long time it seemed as though he wasn't really gone. His BO lingered around for days, mostly in our brains I'm sure, but it would have been just like Rock's spirit to hang around long enough to pay us all back.

Murphy was an interesting character, too, a fucking new guy assigned to my fireteam. To tell you the truth, I don't much

11

remember him; probably because I don't wanna remember him, not really, not after what happened. I didn't even want him in my team. Told C-More I had enough responsibility; didn't need no fucking new guy to worry about. He's dead meat, I said. You can tell, man. Look at him. A scrawny little fucker, pure white, not a scratch on him. We looked over at Murphy. His face turned red. He blushes for god sakes! I said. Send him back; he's just a kid, can't be more'n seventeen, won't last more'n two months. Tell 'em we need seasoned troops. Take him or leave him, C-More said. So, I took him, cuz anybody, even a fucking new guy, is better than nobody when you're short handed.

We named him after Audie Murphy based on his desire to win all kinds of medals. I'm gonna start slow, he said, just a bronze star first, maybe a silver after awhile. Iffin I gotta, though, I'll stay here forever till I get me a medal of honor. I promised my girlfriend I'd bring her the big one.

He was dead serious. We laughed at him, told him he was full a shit. Pointed out that all the medals in the world plus a dime might get him a cup of coffee if he was lucky. Then we took a vote on it and decided calling him Audie was premature, so we settled on Murphy figuring we could always change it when he proved how brave he really was. Problem was, he never got much of a chance, although in a sense I guess he did get to stay in Nam forever. I watched them fetch his boot out of a tree, his leg still in it, the trouser still bloused. I wonder if I shoulda done more; I worry that I shoulda done more. But dammit, he was a fucking new guy, and I told them I didn't want him in my team. They should have listened. He was a scrawny little fucker, pure white, not a scratch on him. He blushed for god sakes! He was just a kid, couldn't have been more than seventeen. He didn't even last two months.

-14-

Whut's gon on Home? ast Watson, strolin' up for chow. Hey brotha! say Benjie, givin' him five. Ain't nuffin gon on, C-More say, joinin' in.

Whut chu be eatin', Rootie, ast Watson, curious. Dates, I

answer. Dates? he laff. Where you be gittin' dates? Back home, I say. From my church sisters. Sho nuff? he say. Sho nuff look like candied roaches, laff C-More. E'body else be laffin' too. I lit a joint, den pass it round. Bout third hit, Watson spoke.

Know whut lock my jaw? he ast. Probbly yo brain, say Benjie, jivin'. Mos' likely he mouf, laff C-More. I be serious now, say Watson, cuttin' eyes all round, then snickerin' he self. Know dat bidness, bout all mens be crated equal? Bout how us splib dudes be from crater, where it be hot, an dat be why we's all black. Whut chu be gittin' at? ast Benjie, impatient. Be koo man, say Watson. Jus want know how comes we not all equal, why dey be blacks 'n whites firs' place, why dey wold be so prejis gen black folk. Wo! say C-More. White dudes be nuttin' but elbinos, man. Be fucked up splib dudes' all. White dudes alway be lookin' fo scapegoat, say Benjie. Goats be white, mos'ly, say Watson. Sheeps be black. Ain' nobody prejis gen honkies is dey Rootie?

Sho is, I say. Dudes be gittin' down on me all my life. You! say Benjie, all credulous. You no be tellin' no troof, say Watson. Why people be gen you? Cause I be Talian, I say. Some folks no be likin' Talians any morn splib dudes. Kids use fight jus' see who gits whup up on me nex. Damn! say Watson. No lie now? You be tellin' troof? The Man be prejis gen hisself even? I nodded. Lord O Lord! he sclaimed. Wold be fuck up sho. Speakin' fucked up, say Benjie, crushin' dope unner his boot. Looky dis shit comin'.

Tenent Little come mosin' up den, disruppin' chow. Rootie! he order. You and Benjie report to Corporal Seldom for shitter duty. O, man, say Benj. We be burnin' shitters all mornin'. Git some others here do it. Come on Benj, I plead whisperin', pullin' his arm, my back to Little. We cleans dey ossifers' shitter, then talk to Mortars. Maybe plant a short round in it nex time the shit hits dey fan. Plant a short round up his ass, he say, too loud neath his breath.

Little look at him mean. I want both barrels burned clean come dark, he say. Benj stan up sudden. You be so all fire up git it done, he say, whyn't chu come stir? Little face round at him square. Gon be bad any second, hadn't Kody come along.

Why are these men sitting around idle? he ast. Get them

13

working, Little, cleaning rifles if need be, but get them doing something. Yes sir, saluted Little. Doing just that, sir. Benjie and Rootie just volunteered for shitter duty. Watson and C-More are going to police up the area, then haul water.

Fuck! swo Watson. Ain' so much prejis gen black folk as gen no rank. Shit flo down till so deep cover us privates' haids. Ebbody laff-n-laff at Watson's play on words. Watson just stan dare shit-eatin' grinnin'. Don' be makin' fun my smile, he say. Smack you dudes silly. Little walk off feelin' tall, fowlin Kody.

-15-

Dysentery is the shits pure and simple. Saw a Corps of Engineers man hugging the top of a phone pole and grimacing in pain as crap, ballooning his bloused trousers, flowed uncontrollably twenty minutes and twenty feet to the ground. Made a cow chip only a masked Hercules could have hurled. Flies stormed the lower half of his bent body, attacking as though they hadn't eaten in weeks, buzzing and zigzagging all around like neutrons in a microscope. One thing we all learned early on was how to take a shit in a hurry. Big green and black flies breached every extrusive act with a frenzied boldness so effective, assholes slammed shut like door-ways to heaven.

-16-

Terry, Mike said sobbing into the phone. Matt drowned today, Terry. My little brother drowned. We tried to save him, he said. Honest. I tried to save him, but – he panicked, Terry. He panicked.

-17-

Hill 602 took three lives the first time. Took Tommy Baker's lower jaw too. I couldn't look him in the eyes that saw so clearly through all of us to the horror we saw in his mangled face. No teeth bestowed upon him the look of a man made wizened with age. He was certainly wise enough to walk out on his own power, though, saving time and four of us the hassle of carrying him dripping blood every two and a half feet for Tail End Charlie to follow in the dusk. Baker died at the foot of 602 as we laid him in the chopper that wouldn't dust him off sooner, when they should have, because the shit had hit the fan. Some chopper pilots think more of their ships than saving lives, said Lieutenant Birch. Economic choices start and stop most wars, explained Captain Kody.

-18-

IMMERSION FOOT! screamed the captain into the radio. All my men got immersion foot. I'm bringing 'em in. Nobody can walk, over. Hold that hill Kody, said the radio. Hold 731 at all costs, dammit. Get that fuckin' flag up. That's an order, over. Say again? Can't read you, over, Kody lied.

-19-

A .51 caliber burst a hole the size of a softball in Roger's backpack. Ham and limablood sprayed all over me. The hole in Roger's chest was only as big as my thumb, but he was dead as I cried Oh God get me outa here. I'll be good. Our Father who art in heaven hallowed be Thy name. Thy kingdom come Thy will be done on earth as it is in heaven. Hail Mary, full of grace, get me home, please, please, I'll go to church. I'll be good, honest, get me home. I'll believe. O my God I am heartily sorry for having offended Thee, and I detest all my sins now and at the hour of my death, Amen.

-20-

Hill 602 took seventeen six days later, and that's when Shorty Premis and I reconfirmed our vow. How come every time we go up 602 we get our ass kicked? he wanted to know. You've heard the rumors, I said.

-21-

Getdown dumbass! You got an immediate death wish, or what? I wondered. Whether he did or not doesn't matter, though. It was a round between the eyes, I think, because as I yelled in his face, it disappeared, replaced with a blood geyser and the sound of a .41 millimeter. His legs slid apart slowly at first, then crumbled in the true Cartesian split. A gurgle rose in my throat; puke splattered my rifle. Son of a bitch. Son of a bitch. I tried to voice the words as the barrage increased, and the tears blocked my vision, and my whole body shook like his leg twitching beside me.

-22-

Say there PFC, said Lieutenant Little. Anyone goes through what you been through must be better off for it. I mean losing four buddies all at once like that has to have made you a better man, a man deserving of a promotion, so I'm going to recommend you for Lance Corporal.

Take your Lance Corporal and shove it up your ass, I wanted to say but didn't, sobbing to sleep quietly that night, remembering our vow, trying desperately to suppress the anger heaving deep in my gut.

-23-

They called it Operation Dewey Canyon. We called it what it was, Dragon Valley, almost before leaping out of the choppers scurrying to set up a perimeter defense. SADDLE UP! WE'RE MOVING OUT! the lifers had shouted. Seventy pounds of gear is what I'm told we carried on average. There were no scales but those on our arms and legs. Jungle rot it's called, and I still bear the white scars on my elbow and scrotum. Jungle rot, born of infected scabs, created more scar tissue than the Fruit-of-the-Loom boxer shorts so few of us wore.

Skivvies roll up into tight filthy knots and scrape the fleshy part of your thighs raw, warned Corporal Seldom to all incoming

Boots. Wear them if you want too, but don't bitch to me when you shitheads can't fuckin' walk.

Found out the hard way he was right, but I didn't bitch none, leastways not out loud.

-24-

Rootie! Rootie! Come closer Rootie.

I'm here, Benjie, I'm here, I said, clasping his hand on my arm.

Help me Rootie, my legs won't move.

Aw Benjie, it'll be okay Benj, I'll give you mine.

I'm cold Rootie, so cold.

CORPSMAN! CORPSMAN! I shouted. Take it easy, Benjie. Breathe deep. Breathe real deep. Come on Benjie; this ain't fair, god. GOD! WHERE THE FUCK ARE YOU! Come on Benjie, give me a chance to pay you back at least. But he'd already died. I knew that I suppose, but I covered him anyway. I covered him with my poncho, and I covered him with my own warmth. Benjie had befriended me early on in my tour. We both were privates which provided one bond, I believe, and we were both from Oklahoma and New York which provided another, even stronger. He died with a death grip on my left arm. It felt like I tore off part of my-self when I finally worked his dead fingers loose.

A crashing explosion ripped apart a three-foot thick tree stump a few yards away. Help! said someone. Help! I rose from Benjie in a daze, apologizing for having to leave him there, and stumbled across a dry, rocky stream bed toward the calls for help. CORPS-MAN! CORPSMAN! The cries were behind me now, and I whirled as a grenade bounced off a rock, rolled toward Benjie's body and exploded. Benjie jerked, and something inside me snapped. The ultimate frustration, I recognized then, as before and again, was that I was powerless to respond to anything more than my very immediate situation. Rage vice-gripped my senses, taking me captive. I ran darting and zigzagging and screaming and crying and firing my rifle and lobbing grenades. All around me others were doing the same and more. There was total chaos in the beginning; then the contagion spread, oil-on-water, as we left in our wake a tableau of death and desolation. A whole village was leveled by fire and indescribably destructive behavior. I remember the smell of burning hooches and the abrupt silencing of baby cries. One by every one of the wailing screaming villagers was systematically silenced as a wave of grunts swept the fire zone searching for weapons and survivors. A dog barked once, twice, then yelped never to be heard again. A decapitated chicken do-si-doed to the music of machine gun fire, rebounding like a blind person in a crowded revolving door. Branches, leaves and straw snapped and sizzled, crying out screams of pain, hissing at death's door. Our voices turned to whispers and our countenances to shame. We left as murderers, our tails between our legs, but it would happen again, inevitably, and each will take his memories to the grave. Life's a bitch – and then you die.

PART 2

IN MEDIAS RES

Terry P. Rizzuti

SURVIVAL

GOOOOD MORNINGGGG VIETNAM!

You can't be serious, Raven, said Bursar. What's so good about it?

Things can't get any worse than this, Raven said, stretching and wiping the sand out of his eyes at the same time.

You ain't been here long enough to know what bad is, said Bursar. Wait a couple more months.

It had been raining for twenty-three straight days, sometimes misting or sprinkling or drizzling, sometimes pouring lightly or dumping buckets, pounding off our helmets and flak jackets, but never, never ceasing. We were on patrol this, the morning of our sixteenth day out. Raven and I had been sharing a rubber lady because mine had a hole in it and his was brand new. It was December, and I was thinking about how miserable Christmas was going to be. The air was cold, my teeth were chattering, the chow sucked. Chow? C-ration leftovers from World War II. The issue date on my box was 1944. This was 1966. We were smoking twenty-year-old cigarettes. Eatin' meals older than we were.

Cut me some fuckin' slack, said Raven, flinging his vintage beefsteak in the dirt.

Police up! ordered Corporal Seldom, we're moving out in five.

We each dug small holes and buried our trash. Somewhere in the distance to the east could be heard the steady, thunder-like boom,

boom, boom of 1-5-5 mm naval artillery fire answered by the distant echoing explosions in the west. We were heading north, having just chowed down. I was point, responsible for ensuring we avoid ambush, and I was daydreaming, thinking about home and what everyone might be doing.

The jungle was thick and silent except for the rain and the clatter of us moving troops. There were eight of us left out of the original twelve squad members of two weeks earlier, nine of thirteen if you count Sparky. A foreboding shiver skittered the length of my backside, suddenly, from the top of my shoulders to the base of my spine. Scared, I dropped to one knee followed by the seven others behind me and began surveying my senses. Couldn't hardly see a thing. Only the rain made sound, splashing off wet leaves. The familiar but rank body odor rose from deep inside my flak jacket and hovered about lip level, a smell not unlike musty mothballs mixed with mentholated sweat. I took a deep breath, sucking in the combined faint odor of burning leaves and betel juice. In the corner of my vision knelt Raven, his eyes stretched wide, his face red, an unlit wet cigarette drooping from his lips. The wind was from the northeast. I took another even deeper breath. Corporal Seldom moved up quietly with Bursar and whispered What's Up?

Gooks, I responded, in front of us to the right.

Okay, let's move around and in on 'em from the west, he ordered. Lead out slowly, Rootie; use hand signals. Bursar, spread 'em out and keep 'em spread.

About five paces apart we half-stepped northwestwardly, my eyes shifting rapidly in search of boobytraps and places of con-cealment. I picked my cover with each step, that rock or tree or stump or hole or log that would offer protection, however slight, if the shit should hit the fan. Sparky let out a low whimper behind me and I dropped again, this time about thirty yards from the corner of a hooch. It was part of a village, and we were in it before realizing our predicament. But fortunately we stood at the outer limit with only a pill-box shaped bagota to our backside, a religious place in which Corporal Seldom quickly assembled us.

The bagota had no outlets except a door with eye-level slits on either side facing east toward the village. Incense burned heavily beside an icon in a recessed corner. We called them bagotas because they were small one-story structures like baby pagodas. Sparky curled up in the middle of the floor looking more scared than I'd ever seen him.

What do we do now, we all wondered?

Rules of engagement be damned, Seldom said. The only thing to do is sweep right in like we own the place. If the shit hits the fan we rendezvous east of last night's campsite about 1,000 yards. Clear? All nodded. Okay, fix bayonets. Rootie, lead out. Everybody lock and load.

We each checked our chambers, fixed bayonets and clicked the safeties off. The incense smell was making me so fidgety I started through the door too quickly and was exposed when a villager appeared from the shadows. His black pajamas, light conical hat and dark weapon stood out against the green background. I threw my rifle to my shoulder but took aim too late as he whooped and bolted through the trees and into the village. I jerked into all-systems-go, but he scurried outa sight.

Very quickly loud Vietnamese chatter spread knowledge of our presence. We swept through the village then, on line about fifteen or twenty paces apart but within each other's eyesight. A bouncing betty sprang, suddenly, ripping apart the stillness and JB's stomach. Why don't people learn? I thought later. Flak jackets don't work when they're unbuttoned. Worm-like creatures spilled out of his guts onto the ground, nightcrawler size and beyond. I reached for a tourniquet bandage in my helmet band. Two more rounds exploded one after the other and down went Seldom, together with Sparky. JB was in shock, his face like chalk, but something told him to stuff the worms back in his stomach. I puked that morning's breakfast, heaving it onto a cold campfire, splattering ashes in front of a hooch door.

Seldom and Sparky didn't move, just laid there in the dirt all twisted up. I figured they were dead. JB! I said. JB! The look in his face was like others I'd seen. Sheer horror preceding death. Morgan worked his way toward me, but I motioned him away shouting BOOBY TRAPS! DON'T MOVE!

CRACK, CRACK, CRACK went an AK-47. Morgan groaned

and went down. Did my stopping him kill him, I worried? Raven lobbed an M-79 toward the sound of the cracks. I ran to Morgan in time to promise him the impossible, that I'd visit his parents and girl friend. He choked up blood, then coughed and died. My God! I thought. But God is boys, and I yanked off his dog tags and headed back to JB who twitched twice a split second before the CRACK, CRACK repeated. Raven fired again and then zigzagged full-tilt boogy toward Bursar, a Lance Corporal and next in command. I grabbed two grenades off JB and headed toward Bursar and Raven. Three gooks jumped up out of a spider trap firing semi-automatic carbines. I clutched my left shoulder, stumbled and stood, stumbled a second time and plunged into a small water buffalo corral, crashing through a rotted out railing. Shit literally hit the fan then. I pulled a pin and tossed one grenade. The gooks ducked safely, but Raven was on target when they rose. Not bad, I thought, for the first time he's carried the blooper.

CRACK, CRACK, CRACK I heard as I watched mud kick up around me and flashes in the trees. I aimed at the flashes and heard the crash and thud of something falling, when suddenly a muffled scream pierced the confusion. It was Ricky, the radio man. I dashed toward the sound right behind Bursar. Ricky was dead, his throat slit wide. Tears welled up in my eyes, mixing with the rain. John and Raven came in then, and the four of us mustered together for a few seconds to decide what to do.

We'll come get the bodies later, said Bursar, when we got reinforcements.

I can't be captured, man, I can't be captured, John repeated, sweat flinging off his face as he shook his head. We bonded that sentiment in one shared glance and bolted back toward the bagota, John carrying the radio, me carrying Ricky's bloody dog tags.

Unexpectedly out came a young woman from the bagota. You gimme chop chop? You gimme chop chop? she said with outstretched hand to John. CRACK, CRACK went another AK-47, this time even closer, breaking the concentration. GRENADE! I screamed and dove as the one in her outstretched hand went ping just before blowing them both all to hell. Bursar and Raven headed for the bush as I pulled the radio from John's broken, pock-covered body and chased after them, my arm throbbing bad. CRACK CRACK went the CRACK CRACK followed by the CRACK CRACK tearing up my footprints as I laid them down.

I ran and kept on running, and I ran till I thought back to high school track and what it was like to run again for dear ol' alma mater. When I stopped I realized I was alone. I was alone in the jungle in Vietnam, eight thousand miles away from home, but worst of all I was alone inside, with nobody but me for company. The one good thing: my flak jacket had deflected the bullet, so my arm only throbbed from the bruise that welled up.

-2-

Dear Me,   22 April 67

I got a letter from my mom yesterday. Do you know what she reminds me of? A textbook – always telling me that war is hell and to be especially careful and that women should run the government so there wouldn't be any wars. Nothing but bullshit 'cause if women ran the government we'd have chaos in every country. In which case my only suggestion is that if women did run the government and war did happen to break out, then women should do the fighting. Then I could sit back and take it easy. What a switch – if you were over here and I was over there. Oh well, it'll never happen because men like to fight too much, they like their women unscarred, and men have the last word. You can tell by the scriptures that men have the last word. You never hear anyone say Awomen Sister. It's always Amen Brother.

We're not in Phu Bai anymore. We're about ten miles north of Hue. Soon we're supposed to go humping into the mountains. They tried to get us to leave our helmets and flak jackets behind. No way in the world this kid's gonna be that stupid. With a name like Operation Kingfisher it's got to be for the birds.

I'll write when I can. Tell everybody hi. Oh, and if my parents will let me, I'll come visit you in New York as soon as I get home. I already can't wait.

Love, Rock

25

Terry, Terry, she said, shaking my foot. Wake up, wake up. It's time for school. You'll be late again. Wake up.

School? I thought. School?

You were sleeping with your eyes open again, she said. It's spooky, Terry, uncivilized.

Where the hell am I? I thought. Oh yeah, it's Monday, I remember. Last night was another twelve-hour shift. How long have I been like this? I asked.

Ever since I've known you, she said. You need help you do.

I slipped out of bed and into my jeans. Why don't you put on some damn underwear, she said. I swear, you can be such an animal sometimes.

No, I mean how long have I been asleep? I asked, ignoring her.

About three or four hours, she answered.

Damn, I swore. How many times have I gotta tell you? Don't let me sleep that long. I ain't got the time.

That's why your eyes are always open, she said. You don't sleep nearly enough.

Look, I'll sleep when I catch up with the rest of the world. I'm four years behind, remember?

More like light-years behind, she said sarcastically.

Fuck you, I said and started pulling on my jungle boots.

I want a divorce, she shouted for the umpteenth time. I looked at her, my nerves on simmer. We never should have married, she said. We should have just shacked up like I wanted to. But no, you insisted on marriage. Said the world was changing too fast. Said you weren't going to add to the moral breakdown anymore.

I looked at the clock. It was late again, real late. I'd probably miss another class. The professors never understood. They just looked at you like your excuses were no different than Fraternity Frank's or Sorority Sally's. Fuck you, I shouted back half-heartedly. You're such an asshole sometimes. You were pregnant, remember? We did the right thing, and you call me uncivilized. Go on, go get your damn divorce, I said, dismissing her with a wave of the hand.

I grabbed my books off the nightstand and my fatigue jacket off the floor. No time to wash up, I thought, and moved quickly toward the front door, opening it to go out. It was raining, not hard, just steadily. Fuck! I thought, mouthing the words and balking at the door.

Serves...you...right, she snapped. I froze at the tone of her voice. She had clawed at the core of my soul, had known it, and had taken delight in it. I turned and stared at her, cold, hard and unforgivingly. The look on her face was one of pride, and she was smiling from the satisfaction of having found the nerve to say that to me, knowing how I felt about rain.

I flashed back to Hill 602, to the time we lost seventeen guys in an ambush. C-More worked his way over to the radio to call in artillery. There was terrible moaning somewhere behind me, but the jungle was too thick and the situation too hot for a medivac. There were ten of us left, but I wouldn't know that till much later. It was pouring down rain, but the canopy reduced the actual effect to a heavy drizzle. I buried my face in the muddy trail, thinking a zillion things like why we were there, why we were doing this.

For the women and children back home, I had told Seldom early in my tour. I'm here for them.

Fuck the women and children, he had said. They ain't worth it, and they don't deserve us dying over here in this God-forsaken waste land. It'd be different if the gooks was chargin' across our own back yards.

I could have killed him right then, right in his tracks, I was so angered by his cynicism and by my own frustration at knowing he was right.

And I could kill her now, I thought. In less than eight fuckin' seconds I could cross this fuckin' room, crush her fuckin' neck, and she'd never even know what hit her. Her smile vanished, displaced by fear, more fear than she'd probably ever known in her life. It was my turn to smile then, and I took advantage of the power laughter has over weakness. The 26th Marines took heavy casualties at Khe Sanh during Tet in January 1968, and I wasn't there to help them, but I'd be damned if I'd lose this war on the home front. I let out an evil laugh and stepped lively into the rain.

It's so easy to be a hero, I thought, when your weapons are loaded with blanks.

-4-

Corporal Rizzuti reportin' as ordered, Colonel, I said snapping smartly in front of Colonel Evans' beautiful rose-colored desk. It was late summer 1968. The time was 0645 and I was in trouble, big time. Colonel Evans was the commanding officer of our Charleston, South Carolina, Marine Military Police unit. He was also large, very large, about 220 pounds, and a combat veteran of World War II, Korea and Vietnam. The left side of his chest looked like a home made quilt.

We Marines were assigned to gate duty, guarding the Naval Base entrances. Sit down, Corporal, he said curtly, indicating the posh red chair to my left. I don't usually mind being gotten out of the rack, he said, but when it's a damn Swabbie's spouse yelling in my ear at 0400, a female civilian for God sakes, that really jacks my jaws. That said, he continued after pausing to take a deep breath, I've heard her story; now let's hear yours. And keep the emotions down; just give me facts.

Colonel, it was 0230, and I was manning Gate Number 3 out at the Strip. Regulations state I'm to check the IDs of all females entering the base after 0130. Only authorized female personnel are allowed: military, spouses and children of military, but no girl friends, no street walkers, etc.

His eyes told me he was impatient, so I tried to run through it faster.

A '61 Ford came through with two couples on board, so I stopped them and asked for IDs. The two men were Chief Petty Officers. The woman hanging onto the driver's arm immediately began hassling me, saying I was keeping them from picking up their children on time. The couple in back were drunk and climbing all over each other. The man's shirt and trousers were open, and so was her blouse. They were oblivious of me. The IDs for the front couple didn't match, so I explained the regulation and asked for the other two IDs. They argued that they were married

28

and that I was costing them money by making them late to the Childrens Care Center. The other two IDs didn't match either, except that the backseat woman's matched the driver's, and vice versa with the other two.

The Colonel grinned as I continued.

That confused me at first, Colonel, and then the woman up front began crying and yelling when she realized I understood the situation. The driver started yelling too and saying I was costing them a dollar per kid for every minute they were late. That's when I made my big mistake, Colonel. I stepped down off the island and said something dumb like, If your kids are really that important to you, you wouldn't be swappin' their mothers.

The Colonel grinned again and motioned for me to go on.

I guess the Chief got mad then because he flung open the car door, pinned my legs against the curb, and knocked me down backwards. I jumped up and ran into the guard house and began dialing for help, just like the regulations state, but when I turned back around the Chief was charging through the door at me. I hit him upside his face with the handset, then kicked him in the you-know-whats. He went down hard, moaning and groaning. I think I may have overdone it when I kicked him in the teeth, Sir. He didn't make anymore noise after that.

By then the others were out of the car, traffic was backed up, the women were screaming, and the other Chief was standing there swaying and leering at me, trying to decide whether to take me on. The arrival of the other MPs helped make up his mind.

Okay, said the Colonel, I think I've got an adequate picture. Your job is to screen incoming and outgoing traffic only, Corporal, not judge the moral characters of the occupants in the vehicles. So, he said slowly as though he were still thinking it all through, because of pressure I'm getting you can either accept a bust down to Lance Corporal, or the first transfer that comes along. What'll it be?

At first I just looked at him, weighing the harshness and the alternatives. Colonel, I said, I can't take a bust for this. I worked too hard for my rank. And if I take the transfer, you might send me back to Vietnam. There's no way I'm gonna do a second tour before people like those Petty Officers even do one.

You've heard my decision, Corporal; now what's yours?

I'll take the transfer, I answered, rising to salute and leave.

As I headed out the door, the Colonel asked me how I knew those Petty Officers hadn't been to Vietnam? I looked at their ribbons, I said, acknowledging his. If they'd been In Country, Sir, I never would have messed with them in the first place.

I may regret this, he laughed.

I already do, I said.

-5-

SPARROW HAWK! SPARROW HAWK! The sound rose like the name itself. MOUNT UP! AND FALL IN!

One hundred and fifty green machines suddenly turned on automatic, scurrying like lizards, preparing for the danger being signaled. Sometimes it was only a drill to test our reaction time, in fact most times, but something about this Sparrow Hawk spelled the real thing. We huddled in the choppers like the scared kids we were, saying our prayers and thinking about home, possibly for the last time or second to last time, or maybe the last time was the last time and this was the first time on the second time around.

Suddenly the two door-mounted M-60 machine guns opened up on the terrain below, blasting away chunks of dirt and stone, the reddish-orange tracers streaking downward like Cupid's arrows in beautiful motion. The significance of the enemy's return fire from the treeline below went largely unregistered as their green tracers wove with our red in an intricate, mesmerizing dance of death. I kept thinking the colors were all wrong, that ours should have been green and theirs red.

Suddenly, I clenched tight as the chopper banked and dove, taking hits in the tail section, banked and dove again, and then reined up and hovered about four feet off the ground. One by one quickly each of us was being shoved out the door. I was first, landed bounced and rolled, my helmet smacking the back of my neck temporarily stunning the whole backside of my head, neck and shoulders. I reached up to make an adjustment but knocked it off thudding against a rock lying beside a claymore mine. I froze for a second, staring for wires. CLAYMORE! I shouted, but the sound was drowned by the blasting of the choppers.

All hell broke loose during the next few minutes as one mine set off another and another and the remaining choppers pulled out under intense sniper fire. Ten of us had been in the chopper that burst into flames from the first explosion shortly after I had gotten out. I had no idea how many others had survived with me. For several minutes it was very quiet, too quiet, like in a dream. I looked back at the claymore. Even though it faced away, as close as I was the backblast and concussion would kill me. I crawled away quickly looking for others who'd gotten stranded with me. For a brief, terrifying moment I felt alone, but then I spotted Raven, his wide-eyed expression telling the whole story in one frozen frame. I bolted across a narrow dike and tripped. Pain tore through my ankle. Limping and leaping like Amos McCoy I arrived beside Raven all out of breath.

How many of us are there Raven?

Just us, I heard him say from what seemed like miles away, and that splib dude.

What splib dude? I asked.

Ronald, the one who just joined us yesterday.

Where is he? I asked.

Last time I saw him he was scrambling over that bomb crater, running like he had something against this place.

RON-ALD! I called just as one of the choppers returned. An AK-47 cracked repeatedly. Raven lobbed an M-79 grenade in the vicinity of the sniper. The AK-47 answered with a shot to the chopper. Raven's M-79 answered the AK-47 twice and then three times. Something green and black and red was dangling from the rope ladder, spinning beneath the chopper like a ragdoll.

It's Ronald! yelled Raven, and he spun back around lobbing four more M-79 rounds at the sniper who was suddenly quiet. Raven and I were alone now I realized as the huey lifted, reversed direction and disappeared beyond the fading horizon. It was a long night for the two of us, hunched up back to back in a dried out dike corner, shivering in the January cold rain, contemplating our lives to ourselves, assuming the worst, expecting no better and waiting for daylight so we could see our way clear to confront the confrontable and avoid the avoidable.

-6-

Dragon Valley was a waterless wasteland, acre upon acre of sterile, arid, wind swept rolling salt-colored sand dunes radiating steel-furnace heat some ten feet off the ground. Nothing moved except small brown striped lizards beating feet so fast they barely touched the sand. Within five minutes all of us were dancing in place, trying to avoid contacting the seared surface.

Ten thousand meters lay between us and our objective, a small but well fortified Cong village, farmers-by-day fighters-by-night as they came to be called. Our job was to close off the back door, the west side of the village. First squad was to sweep through from the east that afternoon, searching and destroying, then pull back before dark. The Viet Cong, it was expected, would hole up till nightfall and then head out the back door for the mountains to the west, straight into our arms.

Traveling conditions dictated that it take us all afternoon to cover the ten clicks. We plodded forth, our minds on automatic pilot, trudging through the sand foot by foot. The heat forced us to use up most of our water, leaving us exhausted by the time we set up ambush. The powers that be hadn't exactly picked the best night for our little maneuver, what with no moon and all, proving more detrimental to ourselves than the enemy.

We dug in as best we could until about 2000 hours when it got too dark, and then settled down for the waiting game. Sometime around midnight someone popped a flare, exposing about a dozen figures within twenty yards of my post. I cut loose with a full magazine some two seconds ahead of everyone else. Another flare popped but highlighted nothing so we settled in again and continued to wait, although nothing happened the rest of the night other than the fact that the wind picked up furiously, blowing sand stinging into our faces like grease popping off a frying pan.

At daybreak C-More sent the Koolaid Kid crawling forward to

scope out the vicinity where the previous night's ambush had gone down. A single sand dune separated us from the area over which the Koolaid Kid scrambled. Shortly after he crested it, a retching sound suddenly put everyone on greater alert, and within seconds a smoke flare popped generating a mushroom-shaped red smoke cloud up over the dune, which was quickly swept away into the distance.

We rushed to Koolaid's assistance only to find him hunched over and puking his guts out violently. Scattered all around him lay the partially interred bodies of what appeared to be two or three civilian families that had fled, we surmised, the terror of our own troops, and were seeking safety in the mountains to the west. In the darkness and our haste they had met the uncaring June Bug Principle. All save one that is. For there beside Koolaid, and the cause of his upheaval, lay a small infant quietly sucking its dead mother dry, clutching her long black hair in its tiny fingers, wriggling its naked body on top of the warm sand, searchingly gazing skyward out across its mother's bosom toward the light blue expanse.

I looked over at Raven and to my amazement a large tear rolled out the corner of his left eye, over and off his cheekbone and dropped to the thirsty sand. Fuck this green son-of-a-bitch, he said, fuck, fuck, fuck it, and he walked off toward the village.

-7-

Hey G.I., said the little kid, you numbah 1. You gimme chop chop I get you boom boom my sister.

But I don't wanna boom boom your sister.

Oh G.I., you numbah ten, you numbah ten.

I number ten? Okay, you number two.

His face immediately spread into a wide grin. Vietnamese kids always seemed so pleased at being told they were number one or two, never suspecting the American pun.

Hill 602 was far from number one but close to Highway 1, a blacktop road running north and south the length of Vietnam along the coast. Somewhere between Da Nang and Phu Bai just north of Phu Loc was a blockaded blacktop road running west up Hill 602. Besides Highway 1 it was the only other paved road I saw in Vietnam other than city streets. Gazing up Hill 602 from Highway 1 you could see buildings, not hooches or huts, but buildings, real buildings like back home. Every time I asked what was up there I got standard answers, rumors actually.

It's an R&R center for top North Vietnamese brass, said Pete.

What are you talking about, top Viet Cong brass? I asked.

The story I got, he said, is that the South Vietnamese government is so concerned that after the war there'll be no place left that isn't totally fucked up, they've designated Hill 602 as off limits to the war, sort of like the DMZ. The North Vietnamese Regulars are aware of the situation, so they've decided to use it as a forward listening post, and have since designated it an R&R Center. Anyway, the gist of the story boils down to this: no one's allowed to go up there but they keep trying. Those who've tried haven't come back. That's why there's only rumors. It's supposed to be gorgeous up there, though, complete with the latest facilities and some of the foxiest lookin' French women goin'. There's also supposed to be some of the baddest dudes ever lived handling security. I heard that Ho Chi Minh himself takes breathers there.

I don't know, you guys. I don't get it, said Mack. Why don't they just bomb the damn place? You know, accidentally on purpose. Nobody be wantin' to lose their stinkin' wings, I guess. You know, those guys get hazardous duty pay. Can you believe that crap? As though it ain't hazardous for us down here. Shit man, I be so tired of this shit. Man, I wanna go home. I be givin' anything for a million dollar wound. Right here. You know what I mean? Right here, he said, pointing at the inside of his left thigh. As long as it ain't right "here" you know. I wanna be able to put out and everything. Like any red-blooded American.

I looked at him, smiling. Mack was built like a truck. That could have been his real name, I suppose, but I never thought to ask.

How bout it Rootie? he said. How bout shootin' me next time they be a chance? You know, make it good so I be goin' home.

No way Mack, I said. We need you man. You're our best corpsman. And stop talkin' shit, man, 'fore it comes true.

Aw Rootie, said Pete, you don't really believe that superstitious bullshit do you?

Maybe not, but it sure seems like wishes come true around here, especially the bad ones.

I'll tell you one thing you better believe in, said Mack: Beware the Ides of March.

You too, Mack? said Pete. And we all laughed.

By the way, Rootie, when be the last time you took one of these? Mack said, changing the subject and handing me a large orange malaria pill.

About two or three weeks ago, I answered.

Start asking for them each week, he said. I don't wanna be reminding you so much.

Okay Doc, I said, feeling sheepish, but I'd rather get malaria than put up with this shit.

Not while I'm the Doc, he said.

The silence was broken by an explosion somewhere behind us, further up the hill we were defending. Just as suddenly the cry went up. CORPSMAN! CORPSMAN! Mack rose, grabbing his bag at a dead run. Pete and I held our positions in case it was a diversion. The path Mack chose ran straight behind us some thirty yards before breaking out into a clearing. The cries came from an angle, however, and Mack chopped off the distance by dashing through the woods toward the sounds. Five or six steps off the path, between two vine-wrapped trees, he tripped a boobytrap just before his screams and the explosion suddenly drowned out the cries for a corpsman.

I got to him as fast as I could, but his pant leg was soaking up blood fast. Jesus! I said, as I tore it open with my K-Bar. Jesus! Blood was gushing in spurts, shooting a good foot and a half with each heart beat, spraying all over my hands getting sticky, staining the leaves all around us a thick, deep burgundy brown.

Leeches began swarming around the blood like thirsty souls at a lost oasis. Mack was writhing in pain, but he rose to look and quickly stuck his thumb in the hole in his left thigh. Hurry! he said. Hurry! It's an artery! And as he talked me through what I needed to do, he was smiling. I was confused. I be going home, he whispered leaning back. It's a million dollar wound.

-9-

Damn it, Rootie, you gotta do this for me. I'm too short be goin' out there no more.

But C-More, I said, I might cripple you for life.

Better be cripple than dead, he said. You my frien', man, come on. Just smash down hards you can. No trigger finger, no bush.

But C-More, I pleaded, what if they make you go anyway, make you shoot left handed?

Damn it Rootie, I gotta get somebody else here do it? I gotta ask one of these others here do it? Man, you my best frien', man, my partner.

I looked around the Quonset hut. Four guys sat playing bid whist in one back corner; six huddled in the other playing no-limit poker. Across the aisle from us, a mean game of craps held the undivided attention of several onlookers. The shooter had that hungry, fire-fight intensity in both his eyes.

But whatta we gonna tell the corpsman? I still hedged. How we gonna explain it?

Shit man, he said. That be easy. I'll just say it got step on or somethin'.

C-More was my squad leader. His real name was Clarrence Higgons and he was from Pennsylvania, from a small town called See-More, which is what everyone in the company called him. C-More had charisma. Everybody liked and respected him, par-ticularly the other blacks who also looked to him as "real" leader. He was twenty-two years old, with a wife to think about and a kid he'd never seen. With only three months left in his tour, he was scared he'd get killed or hurt bad before he went home. What he was asking me to do was take a rifle butt, slam it down on his fist, and smash the knuckles and fingers so bad he wouldn't be able to handle a rifle.

We were in the rear, if you could call it that. There really wasn't any rear in Vietnam. There were just places a little more safe than others. We were in Phu Bai. C-More had been drinking Vietnamese booze all day, guzzling it straight and getting more and more anxious and depressed the closer he came to the bottom of the bottle. The idea of smashing someone's hand wasn't new to me; I'd seen it done before; still, I didn't relish the thought of white bone against a background of red blood and black skin. Splib dudes always scared me more when they bled. Wounded white dudes were simply fleshy looking to me like raw fish. Wounded black dudes on the other hand, their ripped open skin had a peeled away look to it like deep, grill-scorched filet of sole. Something about bright rich red on a rough black background had been bothering me a great deal for a couple of months and I hadn't been able to pinpoint the reason.

C-More slip-dropped the empty whiskey bottle and handed me an M-14 with a look that half said Please and half said This Is An Order. I removed the magazine and cleared the chamber as C-More laid his closed, thumb-to-the-side right fist, fingers down, on the top of the three-step entrance to the barracks. His grin was strained, but wide; his left front tooth gleamed gold in the moonlight. Crusted red dust caked his face; clear spots circled his eyes where he'd been rubbing 'em.

Now, he said, as everyone gathered to watch me raise the M-14 by the barrel and bring it down hard like the strong men do the sledgehammer at the Carnival trying to ring the bell. I made my move, and then C-More grabbed his hand and stuck it under his left arm pit as he leapt and danced and called me a son-of-a-bitch. By the time he had settled down to a respectable SHIT, SHIT, SHIT I had already figured out that my last-second hesitation had been just enough to spoil the mission. He might have killed me right there and then had the rifle not been empty, so I promised and begged to do it right the next time and did.

Three days later C-More, waving his bandaged hand, thanked me profusely under his breath. I read his lips as he stood watching us head out for the boonies on Operation Prairie II. Twenty-six unarmed men on their flight home out of Da Nang had crashed in the mountains to the south of us. By the time we got to them, four days later, the carrion-littered mountain stood wafting ill wind in the form of a dense cloud. Many nouveau riche were made that day, as was a rise in Combat Neurosis.

-10-

Hey Rootie, said Shorty, where's Recon going tonight?

I don't know, I said, and I don't think I've ever seen so many together at once like this. They sure can be spooky looking with that grease paint on. Usually there's just a few of them, five or so. Tonight it looks like a whole platoon.

Yeah, said Shorty. There's forty-three. I counted them.

-11-

From the bottom of the Mekong Delta
To the top of the DMZ.
We will fight our country's ignorance
Any way that'll set us free.

What makes you tick, Raven? I asked, interrupting his song. Why are you so sickening all the time?

Fuck 'em if they can't take a joke, he said. This place is no-where man, the absolute cesspool of the earth. When people all over the world flush their toilets here's where it all winds up. Man, why should I be moral? I didn't ask to come here; I was drafted. *Those* assholes yanked me outa school. *These* assholes don't even want us here. You know that, Rootie. Hell they charge us a fuckin' dollar for a lousy watered down Coke, sell us bread loaves full of tiny dead ants. You damn right I'm sickening. That's how I put up with this insanity all around us, by acting more craziest than anybody else. The crazier I act the braver I feel. Shit, you're one to talk, man, walking point all the time, and at night too. How do you put up with it? How do you justify it all, Rootie? What keeps you from going AWOL? Why not just pack up and head west? We got enough money and ammo to make it all the way to Europe.

I'm too chicken to desert, Raven, so I day dream. I drift off into another world, a world I can deal with, a world in the past. I think about home and going home. I think about high school and all my friends. I think about football, and basketball, and track. Man, couldn't nobody run the hundred like me. By ninth grade I was the fastest kid in the whole school. That was important to me, and I think about how proud I felt. This stuff over here is sick shit, a cosmic joke. It's not real except when the shit hits the fan. I live in my day dream world. I spend most of my time there just biding time. I got 216 days to go, then I'll be free again. Right now I'm only free in my day dreams...

Oh God, I remember thinking as the phone slipped from my hand, bounced once off the kitchen counter, then again off the floor, dangling and spinning at the end of its unraveling cord. Not Matt, I thought. Not Matt. I shuffled into the living room and threw myself sprawling across the couch, then sprang immediately back up. Matt was my support, the friend I told all my secrets to. I can't live without him, I thought, fighting back the tears and the anger. What am I to do?

Both my parents strolled up from the orchard as I blew through the side garage door, slamming it once upside the brick exterior and again as it flew closed. I remember them yelling at me to stop, to come back, as I mounted my bike and headed down the driveway, pumping steady the length of the pavement, turning left onto Hoag Road heading toward Highway 365 and the city of Rome. I pumped it hard, to and through the S-curved wooden bridge up and over the railroad tracks, furiously cranking up speed, the tops of my thighs burning bad, worse than ever before, my vision blurring in the wind blowing against my face. Then, when I reached 365 and stopped, I remember falling on the shoulder in the gravel, tears and snot pouring all down my face, cramps gripping both my legs and left side, the sun battering the back of my sweaty neck. Why Matt? I wondered. Why not me? I asked out loud...

But that's dangerous, Rootie, sittin' around dreaming all the time. Some gook's gonna sneak up cut your nuts off sometime.

I don't think so, Raven. I'm amazingly aware when I'm dreaming. Oh sure, I don't pay a whole lot of attention to following people's conversations. But I can tell you who's where and doing what. I can spot any kind of movement out of the ordinary, out of the pattern. My sense of smell is real good. That's why I walk point, Raven. Not because I like it up there or because it's fun. But because I feel safer, more in control. It gives me my only sense of power. Does that make sense?

No, I figured you was just a crazy fuckin' gyrene, Rootie, like the rest of us. I figured you didn't have no brains, just a dumb leatherneck.

Hell no, Rave, that's only part of it. I can smell 'em, man. Gooks stink to me, like burnt leaves and betel juice. I think I'm allergic to 'em. I can smell 'em anywhere, especially in the boonies. Besides, this is *my* life here. I don't want nobody else in the driver's seat, you know what I mean? If I'm gonna get dinged I want it to be 'cause of something I did, not 'cause some tired-ass Boot walked us into an ambush, or because somebody suddenly feels brave enough to go on the offense and jeopardizes all of us. I'm on defense, Raven, 100 percent all the time. I got one job to do here – get my young ass home in one piece, and I hope I can take the rest of us with me in the process. That's it, man. That's the absolute bottom line. The only thing that might stop me is the June Bug Principle.

We're just alike that way, Rootie, but I'm on offense. There's something inside me I don't understand. I get off on the rush, and it's only when the shit hits that I get a chance to learn what it is. I gotta kill, murder, burn and plunder. I gotta remove myself of any and all obstacles to my survival. If that means killin' women and children I'll do it. If it means burning villages I'll do it. If it means cuttin' off some gook's balls and stuffin' 'em in his mouth I'll do it. If I gotta take an ear I'll take an ear. Whatever I gotta do to tame this adrenaline I'll do, even if it means murderin' some tightass second lieutenant.

You're sick Raven, but I'm sure glad you're on our side.

Yeah, he said. The world's a big pussy – fuck it.

-12-

Hey dude, whatchu be doin' my bed no clothes on? Hey dude, get yore ass out my bed dude, get out.

I rose to discover myself sprawled across the foot of some splib dude's bed, my feet toward his head. He was yelling at me to get out of his rack. I was stark naked. Not a stitch on. He kicked at me from under the covers to get out. It was dawn and I was slow to piece it all together – the night before and what brought me to this bed kitty-corner across the squadbay from my own bunk. I was hungover bad this, my eighteenth day at Camp Lejeune, North Carolina, less than a month and a half after returning States-Side. I stared at my clothes, a pile lying on the floor next to my bunk. Glancing back at the splib dude I realized that only his own embarrassment of having a naked honkie in his bed prevented his kicking my ass up one end of the barracks and down the other.

I staggered to my clothes to find the pockets and my wallet empty, trying hard to remember whether I had spent everything the night before. Flashes from the past seventeen days shot through my brain as friends gathered around to fill me in on last night's series of events. Tony Stagliano and I it seems had slugged Singapore slings in a contest of manhood at the NCO club. We were tied at thirty apiece when the next round of six drinks arrived. We were ordering by sixes because the service was slow. Then, when tied at thirty-two apiece, Tony's face smashed his glass and the table hard, his nose spewing blood in a pool beneath him, the glass spinning outward and away, the centrifugal force spilling ice out on the table.

I remember staring at his head down on the table, reminded of the time he'd bowed it in shame before me and the old woman who'd spit on me in the New York City Port Authority. We were on our way upstate to Rome when she'd confronted us in a gathering crowd, shouting Baby Killers, Baby Killers, and then she stepped up close and spit on my uniform. Tony started pacing back and forth, yelling Let's take her ass out, man, Let's take all these fuckers out right here, but something instinctive told me she was right and I pulled him away, saying She ain't worth us doing no

41

more time, man. She's probably forty fuckin' years old and don't know no better. He bowed his head and shook it slowly side to side. I put my arm around him and led us through the staring crowd that parted to let us pass.

A cheer rose from the onlookers as I slurped at number thirty-three while reaching for Tony's last untouched drink. The NCO club was overcrowded and hot. A lot of jamming was going down. Everything was in slow motion and fuzzy. I remember staring at the waving dance floor, at the convection currents of mist-like smoke and at a splib dude juking it with a white woman. I thought back to what Malcolm had said to me that morning ending a four-teen month bloodbrotherhood friendship.

Drink number thirty-four guzzled down fast, and another cheer rose as did I to stand on top of the table. I remember screaming NIGGERS SUCK as a hush filled the room before total silence like a wake. It was early January 1968 and not exactly the most intel-ligent thing to say. Assholes and elbows flew every which way as black and white squared up opposite one another. The table came out from under my feet and I scrambled and crawled and fought to the door. The last thing I remember before hearing "Hey dude, get yore ass out my bed" was stumbling in the general direction of the barracks.

Seventeen straight nights I had arrived back at the barracks in some similar condition. It was then that I decided to stop drinking. It was then that I recognized I had a serious problem. It was then that I turned my attention to getting out of the Crotch. It was then that I realized nobody else was gonna help me straighten out my life, not my parents, not friends, and certainly not the Marine Corps. I was alone again I realized, but this time things were looking up – nobody was shooting at me.

-13-

Dear Me,   2 Nov 66

You'll have to excuse this paper but it's been sitting out in the rain all day. I sure hope I get some mail soon 'cause it's sad watching everyone else open letters when I don't get any. Oh well, at least I don't start bawling like some of these other dudes do.

Yesterday I went out on patrol all day, and last night we set up an ambush in pouring rain. Then this morning we searched out a big village but didn't find anything. Still haven't fired a shot. Most of the villagers were Catholic much to my surprise. They had all sorts of religious objects in their huts. It was weird as hell searching the churches too. I kept telling the people "I didn't ask to do this but it's my job." They don't understand anyway. This is a dirty place and a dirty job. I haven't been able to shave for the past six days, or shower for that matter. I've only got one change of clothes and we'll probably be on top of this hill two more weeks minimum. At least once a day I get soaked to the skin, and at least twice a day I nearly suffer from heat exhaustion. The nights are rainy and cold, and the rice paddies are murder on the feet. Sounds pretty depressing don't it?

My mom's sending me my camera, I hope. The scenery around here is beautiful. I'd like to get a picture of one of these helicopters as it's dropping us water and chow. It's funny but about once a week the S.P. (Shore Patrol) brings us boxes of candy, cigarettes, gum, etc. We even manage to get beer and soda supplied to us. You have to buy it though. And some day when I get a chance I'll send you some of this screwed up money we use.

My birthday's this month and I laugh whenever I think about what I'll be doing that day – traipsing through some mud and getting shot at probably. Well, it's getting pretty dark so I guess I'll see ya. Take care.

Love, Rock

-14-

October 1966, my first night on hole watch, I trembled in fear of an enemy assault on the hill we were defending just north of Phu

Loc, off Highway 1. Corporal Surly, Lance Corporal Higgons and PFC Premis were asleep in the makeshift tent we had erected just before dark several hours after humping up this 400 foot hill and setting up a perimeter defense post at the top.

Every inch of my body stood at attention, staring and listening into the darkness, through which no light or sound penetrated. I released the safety on my M-14, set up the bipods and waited. A tinkle sounded in the blackness beneath me – I strained to listen, my ears pricking out like antennae. Soon another tinkle, and another and then a rattle like tin cans scraping across rocks. My whole being screamed red alert. I remembered back to boot camp and what I'd been taught about maintaining security by not giving away my position.

Slowly, in silence, I pulled the pin on a grenade and clenched it with all my strength. The sounds got closer and still closer until my heartbeats grew louder than the sounds were. I imagined an entire regiment of VC beneath me before tossing that grenade. I heard the ping and the thud and the sounds stop and then resume, but no explosion. My earlier fear was nothing compared to now as I pulled the pin on a second grenade and lobbed it toward the sounds that ceased immediately following the ping and the thud that should have resulted in an explosion but didn't. The rattlings got so close, I thought I could reach out and touch them. I remember thinking that no one had told me a grenade could be disarmed during the four or five seconds it takes to explode. Quickly I lobbed a third grenade, grabbed my M-14 and fired a four- or five-round muzzle-flashing blast into the darkness, but still no explosion.

The whole camp came alive, but no firefight ensued. Corporal Surly listened to my story and then explained it simply – JUST A BOOT SIR – to the lieutenant standing above us higher on the hill, chewing my ass out royally for giving my position away with the muzzle flashes from my rifle. I was embarrassed and angry, and Shorty Premis took over hole watch during the next several hours while I slept. Probably an animal rummaging in the C-ration cans we tossed down there earlier, said Surly. Grenades, he explained, were made for World War II. Most of them are duds.

Sometime around three or four a.m. Shorty tapped my boot to wake me up for a second watch. I stooped through the tent flap, straightened up and stretched, trying hard to snap the kink out of my neck. Turning to stoop back down for my rifle I noticed a tree stump just beyond the tent and slightly below on the hillside. I remember thinking "I don't remember a tree stump there" when it rose, suddenly, towering against the skyline in complete silhouette. It was a bear not five feet away, and its huge snout was sniffing, no sucking the air. He lumbered downward as I dove for my rifle and came up firing on automatic, two, three-round bursts that both missed but brought the camp to its feet again as I again tried to explain myself to an extremely angry lieutenant chewing me out for giving away my position.

No one really believed there was a bear of course. Some of these guys had been in Nam a whole three months and "never seen no bear." I was a boot so it was all in my imagination. Lance Corporal Higgons was embarrassed to have me in his fire team. Besides us, there was only Shorty Premis. Ideally there'd be four on a team, but like most jobs we were short-handed. The last thing Higgons needed for a replacement was a boot, and a white boy at that, a Chuck dude as he called me.

We left on company patrol to sweep an adjacent valley a few days later. While we were crossing a stream a sniper picked off our point man and corpsman and then retreated up a mountain trail. Lieutenant Birch ordered us up the trail after him. The sniper turned out to be two snipers who set up an ambush some two hundred feet up the trail. Our squad walked point right into the ambush. Chris Christofferson, our radio man, took a bullet in the left shoulder. I remember trying to hide behind a slender sapling, as though that would protect me, and trying hard not to stare at the nasty wound in Chris' shoulder and his broken, twisted arm. He was in tremendous agony but then so was I. This was my first sight of so much blood; its deep bright color was absolutely mesmerizing. My initiation in Nam was advancing toward completion. I realized for the first time I had a neurotic anxious desire to stay alive. Never before had staying alive been so important. I squirmed in place struggling desperately to become any other particle of the environment, to transcend the present. The thought of dying so far away from home without getting one last chance to see my family was absolutely paralyzing.

Two weeks later at dusk, exhausted, we found our way back to camp. The rains had washed down our shelter, so we rebuilt it on higher, flatter ground. That night Corporal Surly ordered us all to sleep, not posting a watch. I remember thinking that strange and was frightened. Soon I would become like the others, crazier and more prone to risk taking, more tuned to the deterministic philosophy that my turn to die would come when it was my turn, not before not after. Four of us squeezed into the tent to sleep.

Sometime during the night I woke from a full bladder and stole from the tent to the treeline to take a leak. I thought about making my way to the piss tube, the sawed-off 105 mm artillery shell that had been planted nearby as a makeshift urinal, but I didn't want to make a lot of noise looking for it. Then, standing there hosing the bushes I suddenly became conscious of that bear. Goose pimples coursed over every inch of my body in wave-like shudders, raising hard lumps the size of BBs on both my arms and legs. Quickly I shook it off peering all around, tucked it away gently and buttoned the flap. Seeing nothing, I crept back into the tent and lay there thinking of that bear. Moments later something began scratching the top of the tent. I felt all around me in search of my rifle but only came up with Shorty's .45 automatic.

Slowly I stuck my head out the tent low to the ground, rotated upward, and peered into a dull soupish sky. Inching out the flap I turned, rose and stood facing backward over the top of the tent. There, just a few feet away stood that bear facing me straight on, his outstretched paws raking long claws ever so lightly across the tent peak toward himself as though teasing me and those inside the tent. Thinking this was my chance to prove the bear's existence I whipped that .45 up and pulled the safety-locked trigger, giving that bear just enough time to haul ass down the hill as I fired pow pow pow at his crashing sounds and missed. Once again I faced an angry disbelieving Lieutenant. It was then that I swore vengeance on that bear.

We swept Phu Loc the next day, stopping to touch base with the local CAP unit. That night we slept soundly and woke to the first sunshining day since I'd hit the east shore of Nam some month or so earlier. Corporal Surly sent some kid named Benjie and I to the bottom of the hill for two five-gallon cans of water.

Benjie was an interesting character, a black kid some of the other Soul Brothers called Nestles Quick because he was fairly light-brown complected. I liked him immediately. He had a universal look about him, like he could be anyone from anywhere, and he was good looking in a boyish, going-on-thirty sort of way. Except for his black dialect, he didn't have an accent you could pinpoint either. And he loved to laugh, oh how he loved to laugh.

Anyway, nearing the top of the hill and exhaustion I happened to gaze down the mountainside toward the south valley. A single overgrown oak tree rose above the others some thirty or forty yards below. The bear was wrapped around it, surrounded by storming bees and buzzing. It was raking honey out of a nest into its gaping mouth. I stood for a second and watched in awe, disbelieving my luck; then, dropping the water can, I dashed toward our tent and my rifle yelling HE'S MINE! HE'S MINE!

Two minutes later I blew his satisfied expression to kingdom come with a three-round burst that caught him in the V-shaped, yellow marking on his chest. We dragged his stinking carcass to the bottom of the hill, where we dressed him in combat boots, sunglasses and helmet. Stuffing a cigar in his mouth and propping him against a tree, we prepared him for picture taking. Benjie just laughed and laughed the whole time.

I feel like a hero today, November 20, 1966, my twentieth birthday, I remember thinking to myself. Davy Crockett kilt him a bar when he was only three, though.

-15-

You don't ever say anything anymore. You're always so quiet, so catatonic. You're always spaced out, somewhere else, some other world, never here. What's your problem? Talk to me. What was it like in Nam? Say something. Please. Don't you like me anymore, Terry, am I that boring? Is that it? I used to turn you on, remember? Now you don't ever say anything. You just sit and stare and smoke dope. So help me God you're driving me up a freakin' wall. I can't stand this much longer. You're an animal. And it's getting worse; you won't even go out in the rain. What is your problem? You're practically cosmoptic. If you don't come out of this fantasy world of yours I'm gonna leave. I'm gonna pack my bags and leave, right now. And I'm taking Jayson with me. Do you hear me? God dammit Terry. Say something. Anything. My God! Doesn't anything get through to you? TERRY!!

She was stomping her foot, prancing like a white mare. Her mouth was moving. She was saying something urgent, lots of something urgents. I could sense that much. But nothing seemed urgent anymore. You wanna know what it was like? I thought. Huh? I'll tell you what it was like. Nam wasn't real. Not when I was there. Now it's real. Now I can think about things like why we were there, what we were trying to prove to ourselves, why we did some of the things we did. I have time now to sort back through it all: the dead, the dying, the barbarism, the atrocity, through everything I can remember to help make sense of it.

She was packing their bags, closing the clasps. She was looking at me through tears smearing her makeup and oh, oh she was beautiful. She moved toward the door hesitating, looking at me. Perhaps if I stop her everything will be okay again. She turned at the door. The pout on her mouth was moving to me.

-16-

Dear Me,   July 66

I guess this is another of those letters when I'm not feeling so good. I've received my orders and it's just like I figured. I go to Vietnam for combat fighting as soon as I get back from my 20 days leave. To tell you the God's honest truth I'm scared stiff. I'll be here at Camp Pendleton anywhere from six to ten weeks learning how to kill – something I don't want to learn but have to in order to live. Then I get 20 days leave in which time I plan to do as many crazy things as I can think of.

Women and booze mostly. From then on I go to Okinawa maybe, and then little ol' me takes that giant step into hell and eternity. Every night in boot camp I prayed to God my orders would read something else, but deep down inside I guess I always knew I was destined to go. I only hope that when I leave here I'll feel confident enough in myself to know that I at least have a half-assed chance.

Well, take care and I'll write later.

Love, Rock

-17-

Late Christmas night, 1966, Malcolm and I sat half drunk and freezing in pouring rain on outpost duty some ten klicks west of Phu Loc. Try as we would, the routine of bailing out mud and water with helmet liners couldn't be done noiselessly, nor quickly enough to remove the bottom two inches of water in our hole, the top of the water table.

This is fuckin' ridiculous, said Malcolm, tossing his liner out. I quit! Can't hardly see or hear a damn thing most of the time, not even up close what with the rain pouring in torrents thisa way. It's been coming down steady since November 25th.

Don't I know it, I agreed. And look out there. The cease fire's a fuckin' joke.

Fire fights raged in the distance, now and again evidenced by the intermittent faint flare lights and the red and green tracer-rounds flashing on the horizon. Miserable we were, wrapped in water-logged ponchos, sipping whiskey, trying to do a wet joint and sing all at the same time. Malcolm, trying unsuccessfully to teach me how to sing, changed the subject abruptly. You know, he said laughing, that judge was right sending me here stead of prison. This is worse punishment.

I knew the truth about Malcolm, that he was very well educated but wasn't one of the thousands McNamara sent to Nam instead of prison in order to reduce overcrowding.

Remember the time you told your bootcamp story all twisted to

49

Troy Richards, I giggled, that reporter for the Stars and Stripes?

Yeah, he chuckled back. I sure had him going, actually had him believing I was a murderer, and sent here stead of prison. It was easy to do though, he said. In my mind I really did murder that son-of-a-bitch. I hated him almost as much as bootcamp. God I hated bootcamp, he said.

> I hated bootcamp. Of course, I figured that out right away, my first night even, but I couldn't figure out why I hated it. It wasn't just that the DI's treated us all like filth and called us so many degrading names. I could pretty well handle that. It wasn't that I lost my identity and wasn't even subject to this country's Bill of Rights. I could pretty well handle that too. No, all I was sure of was that I'd give things a chance. Not only that, but I made up my mind to be the best damn Marine in the world.
>
> I stayed out of trouble most of the time, proving myself physically and mentally, and never let on to my near state of exhaustion. I focused on one thing – make all the rank possible, as fast as possible, so maybe one day I'd be the one giving orders. Then one afternoon the DI announced that whoever shot highest at the rifle range would automatically be promoted. I lost sleep I wanted to win so bad.
>
> We'd been in bootcamp five weeks when the time came for us to march twenty miles through rough terrain to the rifle range. When I say we marched I mean we force-marched. We humped in full gear as fast as we could, and in-step to the lead of a gung ho drill instructor who wasn't carrying nothin'. Sometimes, in fact nearly always, we had to run to keep up, but I was determined not to mess up because I was going to win that championship.
>
> At the rifle range we spent the first week dry-running. We never actually shot at anything, we just pretended. We spent hours (all day – every day) standing, sitting and kneeling in weird positions with rifle slings specially and tightly wrapped around our arms like tourniquets while holding and sighting heavy, eleven pound M-14 rifles. And we did this in the sand,

in the heat, in heavy, dirty, sand-filled fatigues while several DI's intermingled amongst us kicking butts and screaming whenever they caught anyone sleeping.

I remember I liked to practice aiming at the back of my DI's head whenever I was sure no one was watching. I got to where I could attain a state of oblivion, a state where I was semi-conscious and everything appeared in slow motion – kind of like in the morning when you first wake up and it's not quite light yet but it's not quite dark either and you can't tell whether you're awake or asleep and you're not sure whether it's morning and you've been asleep all night or it's evening and you've still got eight hours to go. In fact, I got to where I could maintain a level of concentration so intense I could make practical use of this skill. I could slow down the movement of my front sight so well, it was actually difficult for me to miss whatever I shot at.

We practiced with live ammo during the first four days of the next week. The actual day of qualification was to be Friday. I practiced constantly, every chance I got. I even practiced moving in and out of slow-motion at night while laying in my bunk. My DI was so happy and excited, but I don't think he was happy for me. He was happy for himself because I was in his platoon and he'd receive much admiration and praise from the higher echelon for having trained me so well.

When the big day came my drill instructor stayed right by my side, not ten feet away. He wasn't allowed to get any closer for safety reasons or I'm sure he would have. He waited on me like I was his prize, though, bringing me water and ammo in between shots and events. "We're goin' for a record," I can still hear him repeat. "We're gonna hit 243." Two hundred and fifty was the maximum number of points anyone could get; any score over 190 was qualifying, over 220 was considered having fired expert. I completed the first four events with a score of 193. That meant if I could shoot 50 out of 50 in the final event I would set a new Marine Corps bootcamp record. Anyone doing so was immediately placed on the Marine's Rifle Competition Team. All week long I had shot 50 out of 50 in this event; it was not only my favorite event it was my best, for I had all the confidence in the world shooting from 500 yards with a rifle that had literally become an extension of myself.

There was a fifteen minute break between events while new targets were set up. The people who did this sort of thing were said to work in the "butts." The "butts" was a long, fairly wide, five foot deep trench, located directly in front of and below the targets. The "butt" men were responsible for determining where each shot hit the particular target assigned to them. If the bullseye was hit, a pole with a red disk on top of it was raised and placed in front of the bullet hole. That way the shooter knew whether he needed to make any adjustments for his next shot. At the other extreme, if the entire target was missed then a white flag was waved in front of it. And we had a special language we used also. If the bullseye was hit the shooter was "disked a bullseye;" if the target was missed he was "white flagged."

During that fifteen minutes I requested, and was granted permission to make a head call. I went to the bathroom for obvious reasons, but mainly because I wanted to clean up a bit, you know, like in *The Hustler.* I wanted to be perfectly ready when it came time to set that record.

All of a sudden, as I was heading back to my position, I heard the most Godawful sound I had ever heard in my life. It was one of those high piercing sounds, one that can only be semi-imitated because you don't hear it often. You simply had to be there. The whole rifle range went deathly still. All shooting stopped almost immediately. Heads snapped, including mine, toward the spot where some lonely private, some long lost soul, some anguished mind blew his brains out in front of God and all us witnesses. Plus, to top it off, I looked just at the moment when that headless corpse buckled and slumped. Automatically going into my slow-motion state, it seemed as though every piece of jagged bone and flesh deliberately and slowly showered down upon its maker, upon me and upon all humanity.

At first I was scared and confused, but when people began milling around and moving closer I recovered somewhat. Off to my left the drill instructor was yelling, "OUT OF THE WAY!" I could see the crowd part, making room for him as he tripped and stumbled and shoved his way to within a couple of feet of the body. I half expected some leadership, but he just stood there and stared, a villainous grin waxing wide across his face. "Wow," he said, "They should have disked him a bullseye."

I glared at him, dazed, as somewhere up above a chopper circled to take away the remains which had been gathered, placed on a stretcher and then tossed into a dipsy-dumpster. Two people tied straps which were dangling from the chopper to the trash can and then the entire thing just disappeared – disappeared I tell you – as though the incident never happened. Everyone resumed business as usual and the qualifying recommenced.

I shot five straight bullseyes while my drill instructor writhed in joy. He was seeing stripes. "Just five more," he said. "Just four more," as I fired again. "Don't get nervous, you're a little low to the right. Just three more. The wind's pickin' up but no problem. Give it a click of left windage. Just two more." And each time I'd find the mark he'd leap and twist in absolute glee. "You've tied the record," he screamed, "You can't miss now, you got the feel. You got the feel."

I had the feel all right. I had the feel so bad I was squirmin'. Just one more between me and that record, that record that had meant so much and then suddenly meant zilch. Here I was, part of an organization that had about as much regard for human life as Hitler. For the first time in six weeks I knew why I hated bootcamp. These people were animals. And not just your common everyday animals, but animals in the lowest sense – vultures that couldn't even wait for a corpse to cool before picking at it.

I licked my trigger finger twice and glared at that drill instructor. There must be a way to put that mother in his place, I remember thinking. He became a symbol of all the absurdities associated with war and the Marine Corps. You see, I had learned something in those final seconds – I didn't belong there. I didn't belong there not because I wasn't no animal but because I had a conscience and a brain, and it seemed clear to me at the time that if my mind was going to be imprisoned it was going to be because of something I chose to do and not because of circumstances over which I had no control. During those last few seconds I learned something else too. I learned that I could pass the military's final test. I could go one step beyond laughing at suicide, I could premeditate murder.

Darting my eyes quickly over the crowd, twice or three times maybe, I finally spotted him and fixed on what I believe was his cognizant face. Rolling back into the prone position I went into slow motion, zeroing in for that final shot all the while conscious of that DI. Then, slowly squeezing the trigger amidst perfect silence, and while totally disregarding the consequences, I whipped that M-14 around and fired. Bone fragments and human juice mushroomed out raining every which way. For a split second I felt fear and remorse. People were screaming and scurrying in all directions. Someone grabbed my rifle and violently threw me over while several blurred, menacing faces rapidly closed about me. Somewhere in the distance and confusion a white flag was waving.

Damn, Malcolm, what's gonna happen when you get back States-Side? Troy Richards had asked him.

I don't know. Hoping they'll forget about it, Malcolm had answered.

I remember looking at Malcolm who winked and squelched a smirk, then at Richards who stared off into never-never land like he was busy calculating the big bucks he'd make on this story, selling it on the black market.

You don't suppose Richards ever did print that story, do you Malc?

Don't know for sure, he said, holding his breath and passing me the sopping joint. He did show me a rough draft once, right before he left for the States. I tried talkin' him out of printing it, admitted

I was just shittin' him, that it was all a pack of lies, but he didn't believe me. Guess the story became more important than the truth. Then I tried to get him to at least take out all the quotation marks. Tried explaining that quotation marks implied direct quoted material and that my memory wasn't worth a shit, but he left them in anyway. Said literary experimentation wasn't his bag. All he cared about was facts, facts and the human interest element.

Well, he got the facts all right, I said. Too bad it was all bullshit.

-18-

Terry, she said softly, coming closer. I couldn't focus except on her lips. I love you, Terry, remember that. Even though we're always fighting, I love you and always will. Even when you're gone and old and decrepit and remarried with six kids, I'll always remember you, always love you Terry. Always.

Once again, what could I say that Dylan hadn't already?

Well I wish there was something I could do or say,
To try to make you change your mind and stay.
But we never did too much talking anyway,
So don't think twice it's all right.

-19-

It was just past daybreak. Benjie and I had been on hole watch for several hours, our whole platoon on full-alert for most of the entire night. I coulda sworn they'd hit us this time, I said.

Nah, said Benjie. They'll mortar us this mornin' and again this afternoon. Just to keep us all wide awake. Then they'll probe us again tonight so's we don't get no sleep then neither. Maybe mortar us again tomorrow, then hit us at night when they know we's really fuckin' tired.

I stared at the pile of Marlboro butts on the floor between my feet, thinking about how nasty they'd tasted and how I'd cursed them all night long, complaining to Benjie about Raven's choice of smokes. I was used to unfiltered Pall Malls but had run out, so I'd borrowed a pack from Raven earlier. Then it hit me: I'd smoked the fuckin' filters themselves, a fact that occurred to Benjie at about the same time. You stupid son-of-a-bitch, he said, laughing.

I looked over at him and said, jokingly, Who you be talkin' to, asshole?

You, he answered. You be so damn dumb, Dude, you probably fucked up your lungs forever.

You're the only one here I'd take that kinda talk from, Benjie, you know that don't you?

Yeah, I know it, he said, slappin' my back lightly. We's tight shit ain't we, Rootie?

Brothers, I said; we's like brothers, Benjie, twin brothers.

I know, he said. You're the first Chuck dude I ever felt close to, Rootie, ever really trusted.

Thanks, Benjie, I said. You're about the best damn friend a body could ask for, too. In fact, you know what? I think me and my friends missed something growing up 'cause we didn't have no splib dudes in my high school, except for a few migrant workers that nobody ever got to know. I can't wait till we get back to the World, get to know each other when nobody's shootin' at us.

Me neither, he said.

I ever tell you you remind me of Matt, Benjie, my closest buddy in highschool?

No, you never mentioned him, Rootie. Ever write to him?

Naw, I said, he's dead.

Over here? he asked, in Nam?

No, he drowned out at the Point on Oneida Lake the summer before our junior year. Nobody knew he couldn't swim except me. He was ashamed of it. I always went with him, to keep an eye on him, but I was grounded that weekend. I blamed my parents for a long time.

I know how you feel, Rootie. I lost my ol' man when I was nine, and I cussed him up one side and down the other for leavin' me like that, alone with two little sisters, and a big brother who didn't seem to give a rat's ass.

We looked deep into each other's eyes and then slapped hands to bond our friendship. It don't mean nothin', Benjie.

I know, he said, I know. But it still hurts like the devil when I think about it.

You probably coulda got you a hardship case, Benjie, and not had to come here.

I volunteered, Rootie. I got no place to go right now.

You can come live with me, Benj. We might can figure somethin' out together, learn what life's really about, how to get through to that big door in the sky we keep wonderin' about.

Let's not be talkin' about it no more, Rootie. I feel like I got no future sometimes.

Okay, I said. We'll work it out back in the real world.

Sure, he said, the real world. And he stared off into the distance. I've struck a nerve I didn't know about, I remember thinking. Need to get back to this later on.

A family of rats ran across the soaked sandbags to my left. I thought back to the games we sometimes played to relieve the boredom, like catching them bare-handed and putting them in side-by-side wire cages, then dousing them with lighter fluid before setting them on fire. Just prior to opening the cages we'd bet on whose rat would get the farthest.

It could get really ugly. Sometimes they'd run in circles, sometimes straight lines and sometimes they'd zigzag like buzzing mosquitos then croak in crispy black balls of stinking fumes and bones. And the whole time they'd screech and squeal at the top of their lungs.

I'd seen gooks experience similar agony when hit by napalm, or by a flame-thrower while hiding out in a hole or bunker. I can still picture Raven dancing up and down in glee like Rumplestiltskin, wringing his hands, his white teeth flashing in the sunlight, yelling YEAH-YEAH-YEAH! or GO, YOU MOTHERFUCKER, GO! or GIT SOME, GIT SOME, GIT SOME!

Rats were a severe problem, especially at night. It took me a couple of days of trying to avoid being bitten before I discovered their weakness. They loved my mom's fruitcake she'd sent me for Christmas. I could place small pieces out as bait in strategic locations, pretty well controlling their pathways and, thus, their destinies.

57

One night we released one on Corporal McKlusky's wiry chest while he slept. He came awake in a flurry, yelling so loud it woke the whole damn camp. Grabbing that rat with both hands, he clenched so tight it squealed and shit all over him. Sergeant Rotan started laughing so hard he rolled off his cot and landed on the community mirror, blowing several lines of nose candy all over the filthy sandbagged floor. That was the first and last time I ever saw Rotan laugh. I mean really laugh that is.

McKlusky, on the other hand, was so pissed he couldn't see straight. He stared at Rotan like he wanted to kill him, but, being only a corporal, the higher-ranking imaginary black metal sergeant's chevrons on Rotan's collar caused him to consider the potential consequences. Of all people, Rotan wasn't worth going to prison over. Besides, McKlusky wouldn't last ten minutes in jail. It'd be like lockin' a lion in a bamboo bird cage. So he pulled and twisted its neck around violently, and then flung the dead rat on the floor by Rotan's feet. Then he brushed the shit off his chest and flung that at him too. Rotan clenched tight, but McKlusky simply grinned viciously, crawled back into the rack and pulled his cover down over his face. Rotan looked at me and I shrugged like it wasn't no big deal. He picked up his rifle and looked back at McKlusky; I quickly calculated the distance to my weapon. Then he turned and stomped out the entrance into the darkness.

-20-

Dear Me,   27 Nov 66

Please excuse this paper but Tropical Storm Nancy has been pounding away at us for three days now and I'm afraid everything is soaking wet, including myself. I haven't been dry for three days and nights, so say a few prayers for me that I don't catch my death of pneumonia.

I must say I was very happy this morning when I received a big brown envelope of yours. You know the one with all the letters plus that song, plus that hilarious poem on plump women. One of my soul brothers (a colored boy named

Malcolm) turned the song into a sensation. He's got a new way of singing it not at all folk and I must say it sounds good. By the way, I've discovered I really like black people. Ever notice how white people imitate blacks, but never the other way around? (I be learnin' talk jus' like 'em.)

My mom sent me two more packages – decent. God I'm sorry about this mess I'm making but there's nothing I can do. Our tent leaks and I'm drenched and it's difficult writing. I hope my envelopes will stick – they're wet too. I'm in pretty bad shape aren't I?

It was good to hear about your possible raise. Just tell your boss your young girlish looks and charms are enough to radiate the office thereby rating an increase in pay. If that don't work tell him I'll use you for my secretary and will pay you more. If he don't want to lose you he'll concede, but then if he fired you you'd be stuck 'cause I don't need no secretary just yet.

I sure wish it would stop raining for a day or two so I could dry off. It gets pretty cold just sitting here with nothing to do. Well, I'm afraid that writing at this particular time is a chore so I think I'll wait till later. You understand. Be cool.

Love, Rock

-21-

It had four barrel carbs and dual exhausts,
Four-eleven gears you could really get lost.
It had safety tubes and we weren't scared,
The brakes were good and the tires were fair.

Well we left Camp Lejeune late one night.
The moon and the stars were shining bright.
Everything went fine up the grapevine hill.
We's passing cars like they's standing still.

Well we went around a corner and passed a truck.

59

Whispered a prayer just for luck.
Then all of a sudden coming over some ridges,
Lo and behold there stood three bridges.

Jesus Christ, Blue, what hit you? I asked. His name was John Blue and he had a chip on his shoulder – in fact, he once told me he'd rather fight then fuck. I believed him, yet there he was looking as though someone had stomped his ass bad. I couldn't imagine that ever happening. Blue was a twenty-five-year-old full-blood reservation-raised Blackfoot who hated people, but for some reason liked me. I think it was because I always gave him room to be himself, never criticized him behind his back the way some of the others did, never called him Chief neither. He had the kind of rugged good looks that drew frequent attention to himself, especially from women. His piercing steel blue eyes, kind of a dark gun-metal color, almost graphite, contrasted starkly with his jet-black hair.

All he answered, practically without even stopping to say hello, was If you're ever driving so drunk you see three bridges up ahead, don't take the one in the middle.

I always remembered that but it didn't do any good the night me and Top Sergeant Turvey were doing 110 miles an hour down a back road in his red '65 Chevy Malibu Super Sport Convertible that had a 327 and a 4-speed in it. The bridge was coming at us fast when Turvey suddenly yelled GALLDAM THERE'S THREE BRIDGES! Drunk as I was all I could think to say was Don't take the one in the middle. He jerked the wheel right just before we crashed through the left guard rail, flipped twice and came to rest on the convertible top in the river bank. The last thing I remember before becoming conscious of being in the rear of a paddy wagon heading back to base was staring strange at Turvey still trying to shift gears. Here we were scrunched upside down eating mud and this dude's yelling How ya get this motherfucker outa third? My first seventeen days at Lejeune were one continuous nightmare.

I remember once when Blue and I had the whole squadbay to ourselves. Everyone else had swooped off for the weekend. Blue had just gotten stripped of his rank for refusing to salute a woman officer and was restricted to the base for the weekend. I stuck around to keep him company a little. The gesture meant a lot to him, and he paid me back by opening up some.

Ain't a woman in the world worth my salute, he said, lookin' for confirmation.

I gave it to him by nodding and saying Sides, fuck 'em if they can't take a joke.

I like you, he said, smiling and backhanding my arm.

I just looked at him. Don't go gettin' mushy on me, Blue; I need stability in my life.

Fuck you, he said, grinnin' big. I think it's cuz you always knew I could kick your ass, yet you never took any shit off me; why is that?

Actually, I said, I wanted you to kick my ass, at least at first I did. Felt like I deserved to be beat, sorta like penance for some of the bad things I'd done, and I knew you were the one dude who could do it big time, I mean like really hurt me bad.

I almost did, he said, but there was something about you, something I felt reminded me of myself, so I asked around, found out you were Italian and that kids used to gang up on you. I figured us minorities had to stick together. When he didn't get a response, he kept on talking. White kids used to beat on me too, you know, until I started runnin' and doin' weights. Pretty soon I could hold my own, and then I got real quick, quicker'n anybody, and could take on the best of 'em. The meanness was there already, I think, mostly from hearing Grandmother's stories about how enough was enough, that us Indians didn't deserve this white man's shit. She didn't say it like that, though; she had class. And then when I was fourteen I lost my little sister to a white drunk driver, and my whole world got fucked up. I was angry enough to kill, but I was guilty too because I was driving us to town that day and didn't have no driver's license; maybe I shouldn't, but I guess I just blame the drunk more. And then Vietnam came around, and it was like an excuse to get even. Or get killed, he added, almost as an afterthought.

Something told me to change the subject, that the last time I got into a conversation like this it didn't turn out so good. But I couldn't think of anything to say except, Maybe I shoulda done the same, liftin' weights I mean. I thought about it, but joining the Marines was my way to prove how tough I could be, mostly to my father. I never figured on killing nobody, though. Made me feel like a murderer.

Not me, he said; made me feel more like a man, like a warrior, like I was doin' some payback for my ancestors, and getting even for my sister. The sad part is I kind of enjoyed killing. Sometimes, most times, I get so wrapped up inside I just want to beat the shit outa somebody, anybody. I looked him in the eyes. He rubbed his forehead. I know I need help, he said, I know it ain't right to feel this way, but I ain't asking these fuckers for no help; I'll rot in jail first. Fact is, I wish they'd send me back for another tour; I might could volunteer I guess.

Why don't you just go ahead and get out of the Crotch, go back home? I asked.

Can't go home, he said; can't face my family, my people.

John Blue was widely known as the baddest dude in Jacksonville, North Carolina. I think I'm the only one who wanted to help him somehow, who knew that each time he got in a fight it took a little more life out of him. So, I asked him, How can I help?

You can't, he said, just stay out of it.

But what about when there's more than one, and they jump you?

Just stay out of it, he repeated.

It tore me up inside, but I did what he wished. Blue had come home wearing a bronze star for valor. Bragged he joined up and went over to get some gooks, to kick ass and take names. Said it was a chance in a lifetime, a chance to kill white folks and not go to jail. Gooks ain't white, he said, but I weren't waiting on no other war. The guys around him would just squirm, wanting to strike out at him, but didn't have the balls. Of course, deep down none of this was really true, but fighting had become his identity, his reason for being.

Blue was extremely disturbed, had a death wish or something. I watched with sadness as he deteriorated on a daily basis, was powerless to step in. For the entire three months that I knew him, not a single night went by that he didn't find occasion to duke it out with some poor unsuspecting soul. He had come to hate the world we lived in so much, he was very quick to seek joiners in his misery. When nobody was fool enough to mess with him, he forced his world-view on anyone and everyone until his challenges couldn't be ignored. He had the uncanny ability to read a person with lightning speed, and to decide just exactly which buttons to push to arouse his rage. Once a fight started, he proceeded to systematically destroy a good portion of that person's face and, subsequently, his manhood. At the same time, in his confusion he had come to believe that his own was uplifted.

Whatchu lookin' at asswipe? Blue said to some dude sitting at the bar sipping a Bud, not looking at anything in particular, but simply lost in thought staring at two lazy cockroaches disappearing beneath a stool.

Me? came the surprised reply, his thumb pointing at his own chest.

Naw *you*, numbnuts, know anybody else in here named ass-wipe?

Say, listen pal, you....but it was too late for talk. Blue was all over him like a bad case of chickenpox, blood flying off his punches, splattering the wood floor like paint flung at a canvas. Blue entering your life was just like the June Bug Principle....there you are floating along minding your own business when BAM there it is like a sixty mile an hour windshield, changing your perspective, rewriting your script.

Blue was a lot like Ronnie, another dude I did time with for awhile. Ronnie hated black people. I never really understood that. Like the four-day weekend when we swooped to Cleveland to spend some time roaming around his stomping grounds. We were straddling a couple of bar stools, slugging seven-sevens, when a black dude came strolling in, wearing a huge afro and a sweatshirt that read I AM THE GREATEST on the back.

Hey Joe, yelled Ronnie to the bar-keep. Get yore ass over here. The bartender came our way, and when he was close enough Ronnie grabbed him by the collar and yanked him up and across the top of the bar. When did you start lettin' niggers in this place? he demanded out loud, their faces inches apart. You never let no niggers in here before I went to Nam, he said to Joe who tried to pull away.

Sorry Ronnie, times is changin'. If I don't let 'em in they close my shop. I gotta feed the folks you understand.

I understand all right, said Ronnie. I understand ain't no damn law says I can't throw 'em out. And with that he moved quickly toward the black, calling out Hey nigga...yeah you...nigga. What's that say on your fuckin' back? he demanded, moving still closer, pointing a crooked finger at him. Huh? What's that say?

What's a matter honkie, came the reply, yo momma no teach you to read?

Ronnie blazed with fury, his face scarlet red. I can read all right, he said. Let's see now, it says I... AM... A... YELLOW... FUCKIN... NIG..., but before he could finish, a black fist smashed four knuckles upside his head, driving him backward slamming against the wall.

For a split second I thought Oh shit, Ronnie's done met his match, but nothing could have been further from the truth – Ronnie tore the place up, kickin' and scratchin' and bitin' and whuppin' up on that black dude.

It was almost as bad as the time John Blue and Charlie Jacobs came to blows one night in Hell's Kitchen, a tavern owned by Charlie down on the strip. John and Charlie never did get along that well. Supposedly their hatred went back to an incident in Nam: something about Jacobs having called Blue a chicken-shit after he'd been awarded the bronze star. Word was he'd hesitated just before turning hero. During that moment of indetermination several lives were lost, including Charlie's best friend Jim Bo. Charlie never forgave Blue. Blue claimed he'd never have hesitated had the dudes not been white. I knew he didn't mean it, just wanted to anger Jacobs even more. I guess everyone knew they'd eventually get into it, settle their differences the only way either of them knew how.

Charlie was about six foot three and around 230. Blue was no more than five-eleven and maybe one-ninety. Where Charlie was bear-like and strong, Blue was quick and agile, mean like a cornered cat. They were jiving each other at first, but then the argument reached the point of no return, and people began slappin' down bets like nobody's business.

> Kiss my ass, Jacobs.
> Looks too much like your ugly fuckin' face, Blue.

The odds makers were changing tunes like medleys in a juke-box, depending on whether one or the other was either hedging or instigating.

> Your ol' lady sucks slimy green donkey dicks.
> Your ol' lady snorts evertime she gives me a blow job.

Several people began clearing out the center of the room, shoving tables and chairs toward the bulkheads.

> The best part a you ran down your old man's leg.
> The best part a you dribbled out yo momma's nose.

Charlie flared in anger, his fists clenching rapidly. Blue just grinned, anticipating the moment of attack.

> You ain't gotta a hair on your fuckin' ass, he jeered slowly and deliberately.
> You chicken livered murderin' redskin, said Jacobs. I'm gonna show everybody here just how yellow you really are.

And with that they went at each other's jugulars like two wild dogs. By the time the police arrived, both were locked in mortal combat, totally exhausted heaps of flesh and pain, growlin' and spittin' and drizzlin' sweat and snot all over themselves and the floor. When the cops untangled what was left of them, Charlie had ahold of Blue's balls like a nutcracker; Blue had the stub of Charlie's thumb between his teeth, two joints dangling by a thread. Both were white as tabernacles.

-22-

Dear Me,   20 May 67

I don't know what you're doing but you're giving me the impression that you think I'm crazy. I'm not really you know. You seem upset over me considering myself bad. Either I'm not clarifying myself or you're completely misunderstanding.

You see, whenever I lose a friend over here I compare myself with his past, with what I know and have seen of him and with what I've learned through the many bull sessions we've had. And it often seems that everyone has accomplished so much more than I, has so much more going for himself, perhaps so much more waiting for him even, back in the States I mean. Do you understand so far?

Anyway, when I see one of these boys get hurt I ask myself certain questions: questions which can't be answered. My dad and I used to argue along these lines. He used to always tell me not to trouble myself with such nonsense. I don't know why I do, but it's just that sometimes I get so wrapped up with hatred that I can't help but question the Lord. It just seems that everything that was ever drilled into me as a child is in complete conflict with the way things really are.

I think it all started when I was about 11 years old. Before that, I always had a definite belief in God. But one day in General Science class Mrs. Putnam started talking about the theory of evolution, about people coming from apes, or even fish. I got so upset I walked out on the class yelling "Whatever happened to Adam and Eve?" Since that day I've waged an inward battle trying to find out whether there is or is not such a thing as God.

When I was 16, Nanette spent about 6 hours on her front porch trying to convince me that there was a God. She succeeded but only for about a month because on July 2nd Matt drowned. Once again my mind was in a haze. I figured that a God wouldn't be heartless enough to take the life of my best friend; therefore, evolution reigned over Adam and Eve.

Then Sharon talked to me about my problem, and she got me believing in God again, but it took her a whole day. Three months later my Uncle Chickee was burned to death in a car wreck. He couldn't get his damn seatbelt off, and his wife was pregnant with their first child, and they were so young and so happy and no – there couldn't be a God. God wouldn't do such a thing.

In bootcamp I met Craig, a guy from Minneapolis. He did the best job of anyone in convincing me that God existed. I honestly thought I'd found my answer. Then I came over here and I'm sure you know what happened. I've lost close friends left and right. So you see most of my problem stems from religion. For years I've sought an answer but can't find one. I want so much to believe in God but I just can't. He's too cruel at times. I haven't been to confession since Mrs. Putnam's class. I vowed I'd not go until I believed in God.

If you'll really read over all those letters where you think I'm crazy, you'll almost always find that my screwed up questions are concerned with God and life over death. All I'm really asking is that if there is a God how does he make his decisions concerning who should live and who should go. If I could just find the answer I think I could solve my problem. So you see, when you ask if I'll let you help me – sure I'll let you, but I don't think you can. If you come up with an answer I'll come up with a loophole, and the whole process starts all over.

Oh well, I wrote all this to make you see it's not that I consider myself bad so much as the fact that I consider many of my friends a little better. Anyway I'm gonna sign off for now 'cause it's almost useless talking about it. I hope you're well.

Love, Rock

-23-

I'm sorry to hear about your girl friend problems, Father Kelsey said to me one day in Phu Bai as I headed toward the infirmary to have my wounds licked again. They had become re-infected, and puss had soaked through the bandage layers and was running freely all down inside my utilities. The company was headed for the boonies, and Captain Kody had ordered every able body along for the ride. Lieutenant Little had just ordered me to report to the Captain because when Little explained my situation, Kody found it difficult to believe that after more than three months the doctors still weren't able to control the infection.

PFC Rizzuti reportin' as ordered Captain, I said, saluting as I halted abruptly in front of Captain Kody.

Drop your trousers Rizzuti, he said, returning my salute. I looked at him square in the eye with a glare that, had he chosen to push it, would have gotten me court-martialed. I unbuckled the trousers which, two sizes too large, fell to my boots. Turn around, he ordered. I was pissed, not to mention embarrassed since there were other officers in the room, but I stumbled around and re-mained at attention while Kody lifted my utility shirt jacket and inspected the wounds in my back, butt and thigh. Get your ass to the infirmary, he ordered. They're infected.

Yes sir, I said, bending slowly over for my trousers, shooting him a full moon on the way down.

My girl friend situation doesn't bother me nearly as much as some of this other crap around here, Father. It's not really her fault that I put her on a pedestal. She's human too, but I just can't find it in me to forgive her some of the stuff she says and does. We're movin' too far apart in our thinking.

Why don't you come to mass this Sunday, he invited. I know it's a Protestant service and you're Catholic, but you might get something out of it.

I doubt it, Father, but it doesn't really matter anyway – I've been saved. He looked at me rather funny till I explained. You're only kidding yourself. There's no God the way you think of Him, Father. You can't tell me there's any *good* reason why we're doing this shit to ourselves. The Greeks and Romans were right about one thing – the Gods are on the battlefield. Look around you, Father. These are your Gods, I said. *Boys*. Nothing but *boys*. And they're dying for our sins. Look at 'em, Father. Take Raven over there. He's Mars, God of war. And look – there's Watson in one of those body bags over there. We just think he's going back to the States. He's Pluto, the new god of the underworld.

You realize, he said, you're headed for troubled water. You're going to have to work this all out you know. It's a lonely life if you try it without God.

Yes, I said, but at least I won't be jivin' myself, won't be countin' on no miracles.

-24-

Dear Me,   17 Sep 66

We left about 2 o'clock this afternoon and have been afloat about 6 hours. There was a band on shore and several citizens to see us off. We all kept yelling for the *Marine Corps Hymn* and just as we set sail they played it. It was fantastic. Everyone was yelling and screaming and waving good-bye to their wives, families and girl friends.

I feel like I'm on a long drunk. The ship keeps rocking and rolling and the engines give it a rough, shaky feeling. So far I haven't gotten sick like most everyone else, but I imagine that once we hit a storm I'll heave-ho for sure. Jeepers, you can't even get in the heads without worrying about some dude puking all over you.

Just before I left they had Catholic confessions and a sermon aboard deck, but somehow I fell asleep and when I woke it was all over. I really wanted to go to confession 'cause I haven't been since I was 11 years old. I figured it would do some good maybe. Oh well, God probably would have thought that I was only using Him. Someday I will go though and see if I can't get back into the religious groove of things. I certainly wouldn't want my children growing up as agnostic as I am.

You know something? I'm not really homesick but I sure do miss you and my folks and I even miss the land already. One good thing about this ship – it's air conditioned. You're probably freezing in N.Y. but I'm sweating here. Take care and good night.

Love, Rock

P.S. - My buddy's got a portable record player and he's got a Roy Orbison album with *Crying* on it. He's got a Joe and Eddy album too. They're tremendous.

-25-

I remember swooping up the coast one weekend with Robert Jameson to his home in Hagarstown, Maryland. *Proud Mary* was blaring on the radio. June bugs were splattering all over the windshield, directions terminated in medias res. They like Marines in Hagarstown, he said, you'll see. Robby, as I called him, came from poverty by my standards. His folks and several other families lived in a big downtown home. They had no hot water or shower, only a tub and a latrine in the attic, and no heat. Froze my ass off bathing in that tub twice that weekend.

I think it's the guilt that bothers me most, mentioned Robby, almost casually.

What guilt is that? I asked him.

The guilt of never having pushed myself to the limit, he replied, searching for the exact wording. The guilt of never having tried to be a hero, never having put myself in a position where there was only two choices: fight or run. I spent a fuckin' year in Nam, and still don't know the answer. Would I fight if really cornered. Or would I turn tail and run. It eats at me, Roscoe. Eats bad not knowin' if I'm really chicken deep down. Eats worse cause I think I am or I would have proven different.

But what if we'd proven different and wound up dead? I asked him.

70

There it is, he said. There's the paradox.

There's the paradox, true, I agreed, but why the guilt? Why do we feel guilty for choosing life over the possibility of losing it.

Guess it comes from being around too many John Waynes, he said.

Yeah but John Waynes get instant replays, I told him. We might not get another chance. And if we do get lucky and become heroes – then what? Does the guilt start all over? Just because you're a hero once, does that guarantee you're a hero the next time?

I don't know, he said, but it seems like being a hero once is better than this, better than never knowing.

Maybe so, I told him, but I believe in Murphy's Law II: In a war zone, if anything is likely to go wrong, nothing will go right.

We were drunk by the time we hit town. Country couples danced intimately to *Hey Jude* playing on the juke box at the local bar where we received a very warm welcome. The bartender insisted we deserved free drinks; people slapped us on the backs during our stay there, praising us as Vietnam Vets. At Robby's house later on, his mom and four other women, sitting around a kitchen table playing poker, rose in jubilation to greet us.

Robert, Robert, said his mom, grabbing and kissing him all over his face. So good to have you home. A big woman she was, preventing his breaking her bear hug. Who's your friend? she asked.

Oh, this is Roscoe, said Robby, Roscoe Rizzo. We're in the same outfit together.

A few phone calls later and Robby and I joined his two sisters, Shirley and Irene, and their husbands, Billy and Roger, and headed for a VFW dance in Wattsville, a neighboring but rival town. The six of us were intruders, only I didn't know it. Shirley, dressed in pink, took offense when the lead singer bellowed:

See that girl all dressed in pink,
Boy her pussy sure does stink.
Yeah yeah! Yeah yeah!

There was at least one other woman there in pink, but Billy

71

erupted toward the stage, punched the singer in the face, and knocked him flat on his butt. The whole dance went berserk. A wave of people crowded the six of us toward the narrow hallway leading to the back door. I was last man out with no one and nothing between me and some huge monster the crowd looked to as leader.

At the entrance I jumped up, grabbed the door frame and snap kicked Monster in the jaw. Blood trickled down his chin out the lower lip, mixing in his stubble. His eyes blazed at me. He swung but missed, swung again and lost his balance. I popped him a hard right on the bridge of his nose, gave him all I had with a left and then backed through the door into the parking lot, followed by the crowd.

Billy grabbed a trashcan lid and started smashing it against some dude's head. Shirley and Irene were swinging their pocketbooks and screaming at everyone and everything. Roger was duking it out with a doggie in uniform. Monster raged toward me, blood spewing out his nose. I kicked him in the balls once, twice, then a third time. It seemed to not phase him at all, and for the first time I felt fear. He came at me like a rhino, head down, shoulders rounded, fists protecting his chin, shouting over and over YOU LIKE TO KICK HUH DUDE? I FIX YORE ASS. YOU LIKE TO KICK HUH DUDE?

A good fifty yards separated us from Robby's car. We backed toward it quickly. I jabbed at Monster till his eyes swelled and his nose bled more. He swung clumsily. I ducked under and kicked him in the balls again. He was inhuman, or wearing a cup. We were cornered in the lot by the car when Robby flung the trunk open. Billy grabbed the tire iron and smashed Monster across the back of the neck. His legs buckled then tried to straighten but couldn't. Roger was on Doggie like stink on shit. A lady hanging out an upstairs window was screaming HELP! POLICE! POLICE! HELP! The girls were in the car yelling at us to get in. Robby jumped behind the wheel. I hit Monster hard, again and again. I kept beating him, harder and harder in a flurry – leftrightleft rightleftrightleft. Suddenly there was that gook, his head hanging on by half his neck. I couldn't stop beating until my arms quit. His eyes rolled and glossed over as his knees buckled further. Billy reclubbed him with the tire tool, then jumped in the car. Monster fell forward as the crowd advanced to provide substitutes. Someone hit the side of my face driving me toward the car. Irene grabbed me yanking me in the back seat. Everyone was yelling at Roger to get in. Robby slammed it in reverse squealing backwards fast laying rubber. THUMP, THUMP the car lurched in the air just as Roger dove in the open front door.

Rocks bounced off the hood, trunk and roof as Robby shifted into first forcing a getaway path through the crowd. I looked back in disbelief. Doggie looked like a bundle in a puddle. Tire tracks led up to and over Monster. A woman, bent over him, gazed up in fear and hatred through huge tears and a menacing expression. Monster made the *Wattsville Gazette* headline news – so did the APB for Robby's car.

And there was thunder thunder over thunder road.
Thunder was our engine and white lightning was our load.
And there was moonshine moonshine quench the devil's thirst.
The law they swore they'd get us but the devil got us first.
The law they swore they'd get us but the devil got us first.

-26-

FALL OUT! LET'S GO! EVERYBODY OUT! ON THE DOUBLE! FULL GEAR, FULL GEAR! LET'S GO! FALL OUT!

People scrambled all around, straggling into formation in various stages of dress. Some still pulled their boots on, others their packs. Still others adjusted helmet straps, slings, belt buckles, laces. Everyone stood shaking in the dampness and cold.

A-TEN-HUT! snapped the Gunny. LOOK ALIVE! LOOK ALIVE! Colonel Bostick has a few words to pass on to us, he said by way of introducing the Colonel who marched up to the front of the company alongside Captain Kody.

MEN! said Colonel Bostick, snapping his fingers at an orderly standing at attention holding a small US flag. The orderly immediately moved to the Colonel's side and handed him the flag.

MEN! he repeated. Recon tells me there's bookoo Cong on Hill 731. Says they're dug in well. Bunkers, spider traps, tree nests, the works. You name it, Recon says they got it. I told General Hansen my boys could make mince meat of Hill 731, and to prove it I assured him his spotter plane could photograph this here 'Merican flag a waving pretty-as-you-please clear up on Hill 731's topside three days hence. Now, he said, scanning all four platoons, you boys ain't a gonna let ol' Bostick down are ya?

A low stereophonic murmur spread inward from both ends of the company formation, slowly at first and then picked up speed and volume as it converged on the center.

NO SIR! shouted Captain Kody, bringing the murmur to immediate silence. My men haven't lost a fight yet. No reason to think Hill 731 will be different. RIGHT MEN? he shouted.

Yes sir, some answered.

RIGHT MEN? he repeated slightly louder.

YES SIR! came the reply in unison.

Colonel Bostick handed Captain Kody the flag. Kody saluted, about faced and shouted: LIEUTENANT LITTLE! FALL THE MEN OUT AND ASSEMBLE THE SQUAD LEADERS! NOW! Little scurried all around like a lost ant.

Less than two hours later choppers dropped us 5,000 meters northeast of Hill 731, a bald, very steep, rocky-topped mountain. The mortars set up and prepared for laying down a base of fire. Second Platoon, my outfit, was to work around to a position on the southwest face. At daybreak we were to assault upward at a slight diagonal moving counter-clockwise. First and third platoons were pulling similar maneuvers on the northwest and southeast slopes.

We moved out at dusk, third squad on point, right after the shelling started: First the mortars, then airstrikes followed by distant artillery fire. They zeroed in on the far southwest base, walking their way upslope, slowly fanning outward east and west, then converging on the apex before fanning outward again, finally converging back in on the northeast foot, at which point the air and artillery fire ceased but the mortars backtracked toward the summit and then down again.

At about eleven o'clock when we were more than halfway to our destination the wind picked up and it suddenly got deathly dark and quiet. The bombardment had lit our way till then and covered the noise of our approach. Now we realized we still had 2,000 meters to confront and no clue as to what lay before us. In one of Lieutenant Little's few sane moments, however, he switched second and third squads, putting me on point and Travis right behind giving directions.

At about 1,000 meters a narrow, slow-moving river halted our progress. Travis signaled to cross it so I eased into the freezing water up over my waist, holding my rifle high. The current was deceiving, much swifter than it seemed, pulling at my ankles, dragging me downstream. I tried to fight it by taking larger steps, but realized that short quick steps provided safer progress.

Halfway across I noticed my faint shimmering shadow floating upstream to my right. Just about the time I was trying to decide whether it looked more like a scarecrow or a crucifix, a distant THOOMP launched an exploding flare that lit up the whole sky. Everybody ducked quick including me, all the way to my nose, resting my rifle on top of my helmet. The water stunk like piss and tasted like refrigerated raw fish. I could feel my eyes stretched tight in fear. My flak jacket and shirt swelled outward and up, trying to float. THOOMP! POP! went another flare. I moved forward carefully, slowly, inching along, feeling the icy water dragging cool against my balls inside my trousers.

GOLF 6! GOLF 6! this is GOLF 2, over! whispered Little in the radio. GOLF 6! GOLF 6! this is GOLF 2, over! he repeated. The radio squelched loud across the river each time he pressed the talk button. GOLF 6, this is GOLF 2, turn out the lights, over!

GOLF 2, this is 6, maintain radio silence over.

The flare whistled loud, reduced to a parachuting flicker, then expired. I raised up just as something alive brushed my leg. Moving forward more quickly now, I suddenly stepped into a shallow pothole and stumbled forward face first. Matt, I thought, as I neared the opposite bank and forced myself up its slick damp surface. Water sloshed out my bloused trousers and squeegeed from my jungle boots. My feet ached from what felt like rapidly developing blisters. I knelt beside a small bush, peered into the darkness, scanned for anything unordinary then signaled for the others to follow. A leech sucked at the love handle on my right side just above my cartridge belt. Son-of-a-bitch, I thought, tugging at my jacket and scratching hard. Got to let it have its fill.

Around 0400 we arrived at our destination tired but alert. I lay shivering on a blanket of dead leaves and grass. Little had spread us out on line at the base of the hill. Several of the others yanked off sopping boots to inspect blood-covered, water-logged feet while we waited for daylight. Then, as the first rays broke through the trees and the birds peeped their initial songs, the assault began, quietly at first but soon rushing around Hill 731 as some kind of intense energy. I couldn't exactly hear anything, just feel it as it revolved around feeding on itself, gaining inertia like the springs on a trampoline. By the time we reached the 200 foot level, I could feel it vibrating through my bones, concentrating at the hinge in my jaws.

I remember stalling at about the 400 foot level. Everyone complained about sore feet. I was leaning forward on one extended leg, massaging my foot and ankle and thinking about home, remembering it vividly, praying I'd survive this nightmarish interruption in my life. Suddenly the whole mountain shook. Huge boulders came crashing toward us, rumbling like locomotives, tearing up trees in their gravitational pursuit. A hailstorm of grenades exploded all around. Two .51 calibers opened up at the same time, slamming chunks of lead into flesh and bone. Travis flew back against a tree, slunk down and laid there flopping like a fish. A rolling boulder ricocheted off another, dropped off a short ledge, skidded a few feet, then crunched up and over Travis like he wasn't even there. People were screaming and scurrying, firing their rifles and picking their way forward through the smoke and noise. I stood pinned, my back to a towering hardwood, staring at Travis, the lower half of his body squashed flat in the dirt. His helmet hung to one side of his head by the chin strap. Blood flowed out one nostril. Both eyes gazed back at mine through cracked, skewed glasses. Jesus! I thought, and whirled around the tree and emptied a magazine into nothing in particular, when suddenly another gun nest opened up, this time behind us. I dove and rolled, came up changing magazines and fired wildly. THOOMP! BOOM! went Raven's M-79, blowing a door in the nest, silencing its occupant.

I worked my way to Travis, changing magazines enroute, felt for a pulse but found nothing. Damn, I remember thinking, when another boulder slide began. Looking both ways, I started toward a safe-looking ledge but hesitated when lead started flying all around, thunking into dirt and trees. Ayeeeiiii screamed a gook swinging down out of a tree wielding a machete. LOOK OUT! I yelled at Marvin who whirled and opened up on automatic blowing flesh off both the gook's legs, which flung outward and behind, sending him face first descending into the path of one of the crashing boulders. Flattened him out like he'd gone through a ringer. THANKS! yelled Marvin just before an AK-47 round cracked open his skull. My God! My God! I thought as I stood paralyzed.

Suddenly a bugle started blasting strange sounds, and gooks came charging down out of the trees by the dozens. Lead was slinging every which way, whistling all around like buzzing high-density insects. I emptied another magazine and fumbled a fourth in place, slammed a round in the chamber and then emptied that one. THOOMP... THOOMP... THOOMP went Raven's M-79 every five seconds. BOOM... BOOM... BOOM it said on impact. I whirled around as Walker hightailed it past me, smacking my shoulder hard. His dark blue eyes were big as pine tree knots and he was heading straight down hill. A bloody white towel tied to his pack flapped like the back end of a white-tailed deer bounding through the woods. HALT! yelled Rotan just before blowing a tight pattern in Walker's lower back, knocking him tumbling forward in a heap of twisted bones.

RETREAT! screamed Little. RETREAT! This ain't happening, I thought, fumbling another magazine in place; Marines don't retreat.

RETREAT HELL, shouted Rotan and pointed his rifle at Little. I'll blow your ass away, you or anybody else moves.

The whole war seemed to stop at that point, take on even less meaning. I inched my rifle around, thinking This is it. He's gonna start some shit and I'm gonna have to blow his face off. I can take him, I thought. I've seen him in action, and I can take him.

That's a direct order from Captain Kody, said Little. We're backing up to regroup.

Rotan looked all around at us, wild-eyed and hyper, rocking back and forth, one foot to the next. An ugly grin curled the corner of his mouth, then flew open like a butterfly knife. If Kody said we regroup, we regroup, he cackled and spun off downhill leading the way. I felt my heart pounding erratically, then moved cautiously downhill backwards facing up. For the first time in my life the phrase "turn tail and run" had meaning.

-27-

Dear Me,   3 Aug '66

Your last letter confused me at first, but after reading it a few times I figured it out. I promise not to send anymore of my free verse. I had no idea it would affect you in such a manner. I've written a few lines of poetry but it's been thrown away because it sucks. It's easier to stick to the free verse style because you never have to stop and search for a rhyme. Besides, everything I write is sad. Maybe I'm feeling sorry for myself but you have no idea what it's like to be training in things which are meant to save my life in a few months. Honestly speaking, there's no way in hell you'll find me the same kid that left home about a year ago. I listen more, observe more, appreciate more, but most of all I don't take an ounce of shit off anyone no matter who he is. You see it's a funny thing and especially scary feeling to be a trained killer. It's hard to accept and difficult to understand but that's precisely what a marine is – a killer. It's mainly a mental condition. We're not physically capable of performing ungodly feats or anything, but then again we're not afraid to take on anyone even though we'll probably go down trying – if you know what I mean.

When you stop and think about it the amount of training

we've had is hardly suficient to make us ready for the battle-field, but something inside tells each one of us that we can whip any Vietcong that gets in the way. I wish I could explain it better because it's a pretty interesting thing. Well, I need to get some sleep so I'll write later.

Love, Rock

-28-

Her breasts were like M&Ms, milky tan chocolate melting in my mouth and spongy in my hand, her nipples like hard candy coating. Her eyes were large globes, shining and bright. Her mouth, so luscious and full, was both puffy and moist. I sucked her lower lip till the swelling slurred her speech.

-29-

It was May 2, 1967, the anniversary of my first day in bootcamp. The bundled up poncho, thrown beside me in the combat-modified Chinook medivac chopper, oozed across the floor, sorta like a bean bag. I strained to open it, my wounds aching. The chopper lifted laboriously and rolled. The poncho tore open suddenly and spread out on the floor. It was Stricklyn. He was dead but still alive. I hardly recognized him. Whole chunks of flesh and hair were gone, ripped off. What remained was porositic and peppered, red blotches oozing blood through still moving veins and organs. One eye was gone, the other dilated wide open, staring and bulging. It burst spewing puss on raw cheek bone. His engorged dick stood at attention. I gripped the seat and armrest with all remaining strength. I forced my gaze to the window, facing my own horror stricken reflection. Our Father, I said, who art in heaven, hallowed be Thy name. Protect me through this toward some greater under-standing. Help me to know what's going on here, to understand what humanity has done, is doing, to deserve this.

O' Creator of all beyond Stonehenge,
Slaken my thirst for total revenge.
Seize this soil un' Thine control,
Lift this burden – Free my soul.

The machine gunner reached over and placed his hand on my shoulder. Tears shot down my face, splashed off a canteen and mixed with my blood on the seat. I started to sob and tried but couldn't stop, anger raging in my stomach, erupting in my breast. I couldn't hold it any longer and pissed down my pants. Stricklyn was one dynamite human being. Besides, I owed him $50.

-30-

Good Morning Vietnam! repeated the seductive female voice. Wakey you selves up, GIs. Today memorable day indeed. Today you die, GIs. Today you all go to die, all go to hell for crimes against People of Vietnam. Wake up all you GIs, wake up hear this. Yesterday 114 GIs die in battle. Lose two plane and three tank. Honorable Ho Chi Minh followers lose nothing. GIs do bad today too. Will lose....

Raven suddenly slammed the voice down on a rock, cracking the case open, spilling the batteries out.

Oh man! cried C-More, what chu be doing dat for?

I'm sick a that lyin' slant-eyed bitch, said Raven. I'd like to plug her leak with a twelve inch deak, beat her lips between her hips, plant her hole on a barber pole. Besides, he added, it wasn't even the one that speaks good English.

Chow down, said C-More. We be movin' out in fifteen.

Hill 602 loomed above us, seemingly insurmountable. We stood at the barricade examining second thoughts. Taking this hill could wipe out the top Viet Cong brass, shorten the war, win it even. Shorty chain smoked stale Pall Malls. Stricklyn sucked on a peeled stick of sugar cane, his buck teeth protruding beneath his upper lip. Malcolm hosed himself down with bug juice, determined to ward off more than his share of small critters. Raven, imagining himself in a mirror, touched up his face with fresh grease paint, carefully, like a woman putting on lipstick.

Check out the pretty boy, said Shorty. Everybody grinned.

Fuck you assholes, said Raven. You're all just jealous 'cause you're so damn ugly. Then he let out a huge fart to put a period on the discussion.

You're one nasty motherfucker, I said to him, and he just grinned.

Heat burned into the back of my neck, and it wasn't even afternoon yet. Salt bored into the cuts on my face and the sores on my hands.

Nine men's not enough, said Wiskey, never looking up from cleaning the big gun. I looked at him curiously, wondering what motivated him to say that. Wiskey was short and wiry, a mere wisp of a man, yet strong, agile and fearless. We called him Wiskey because of his size and because he spiked his canteens with Vietnamese whiskey, not too much, just enough to kill the germs and the taste, he used to say. It didn't seem to effect his work any. Next to Stricklyn, he was the best damn gunner in the whole company.

C-More looked at him funny, too, and sensed he was losing control of the squad. Square away, he said. You dudes call yourselves Marines or Swabbies? We owe 'em. We owe all the others, like JB and Bursar and Seldom and Benjie and Lugar. Remember Lugar, Rootie, remember man? They blew the back of his goddamn head off. Stuffed his balls in his mouth and then sewed it shut. Remember man? Them muthers hung him by the thumbs from a fuckin' tree.

I remember, I said. Lugar and I went through bootcamp together. He was from Chicago. His orders read Bravo Company, 1st Battalion, 9th Marine Regiment, The Walking Dead. Mine read Golf Company, 2nd Battalion, 26th Marines, The Nomads. We crossed the Pacific together on the USNS Barrett, a Merchant Marine ship, crossed the International Dateline and went through that ridiculously pagan initiation together, partied on Okinawa and then landed in Da Nang together before splitting up. He was transferred from 1/9 to 2/26 some four months later, a changed person, more gung ho, uncouth and crazed like Raven but more careless. The kind of guy who'd pick his nose in public and then pick a fight with the first person he saw looking at him funny. He was captured outside Cam Lo less than two months later when we were sweeping the village. I laughed with the others when we cut him down, a sick defense of our true feelings of hatred, fear and revenge. What's happening to us, I wondered, as we stood there stealing glances at each other and trembling in our boots. Malcolm's eyes glassed over and he began humming *Taps*. Soon we all joined in, softly at first, and then louder as embarrassment set in and we just wanted to get the hell outa there.

Dear Me,   29 Sep 66

I know you won't believe this but every word is true. Lugar and I have finally been initiated. We had to slither and crawl naked through slimy water literally mixed with garbage from trashcans while a gauntlet of guys on either side of us whipped up on our backsides with belts and sticks. Then we had to thrust our faces into this great big huge fat guy's bare belly which was covered thick with green ship grease. Then we had to open our mouths wide while some dude poured juicy garbage and salt water down our throats. After I spit that out, someone slapped me in back of the head with a whole handful of grease and said "You have now been dubbed into the Domain of the Golden Dragons." Here's what the card looks like that they gave us:

Domain of the Golden Dragon
    Ruler of the 180th meridian
    Know all ye Golden Dragons that on this
    26th day of Sep. 1966
    in latitude 29° 00′ longitude 180° 00′
    There appeared within my Domain the
    USNS Barrett
    and know all ye that
    PFC Terry P. Rizzuti
    was duly initiated into the royal Domain
    of the Golden Dragon.

Davey Jones, Golden Dragon,
His Majesty's ScribeRuler of the 180th Meridian

Signature
Commanding

The actual card has a ship sailing on the ocean with a couple of Dragons in the foreground. It's Green and Blue and White and Red and Yellow and Black. Kind of like the flag and the races and this green machine all rolled into one. I'd send you the actual card, but if I ever cross again I'd have to show it in order not to be initiated all over again. And I certainly don't want to repeat this experience anymore than necessary.

Well, I'll write again Tuesday which is tomorrow – the day after Sunday. Crazy huh? It's as though time itself were in a hurry to get us there, to Vietnam. Less than two more weeks and I'll be fighting for a living.

Love, Rock

I remember too, mumbled Raven, looking down, scratching the dirt with his foot, the toothbrush hanging from his mouth that he carried with him always. Got to keep my teeth white, he said, protect my smile for the women. Had to beat 'em off with a stick you know, all them women attacking me all the time everywhere I went.

We laughed never knowing whether Raven was serious or exaggerating his womanizing. He was good looking I guess, in that tall, lanky, John Wayne sorta way, matching both the Duke's physique and his cocky self-assurance.

I'm a hundred and ninety pounds of solid savage flesh, he said, nothing but pure sex appeal.

Everybody cracked up. C-More's gold tooth, a status symbol among other blacks, flashed brilliantly behind his smile. We penetrated the jungle beyond the barricade, me on point followed by

Watson as backup, by Raven and his M-79 grenade launcher, by C-More the Squad Leader, by Shorty and his radio, by Stricklyn the Machine Gun Leader, by Wiskey humping the M-60, by Murphy carrying the bipods and ammo, and Malcolm on Tail End Charlie.

The silence grew thick and eerie as though we'd somehow stepped back in time or entered taboo territory. The heat grew worse. I tugged at the front of my flak jacket to let air circulate inside and cool the body sweat that had sopped through the inside of my shirt and soaked deep into my flak jacket, making it seem five pounds heavier. The familiar rank odor I'd grown accustomed to rose to greet my nostrils, a smell similar to mildewed cardboard. I popped a salt tablet and swallowed it dry, not wanting to waste the precious water necessary to wash it down.

Suddenly, a peacock-sounding bird screamed, scaring the shit out of all of us diving for cover. A path, an old intermittent stream bed, led up through an undisturbed canopy, foliage that hadn't ever seen human trespassers it seemed. There was no litter anywhere, no C-ration cans or paper wrappers. There was no breeze either. Then, a slight gurgling sound arrested our movement. It was water, finally, a creek, a small river really and a six foot tall waterfall in a gorgeous clearing through which we passed single file stopping to take in its magnificence, to suck up the beauty and serenity of it all, and to fill our helmets with the liquid that felt so good pouring over our heads. Lazy fish glided through the crystal clear green-tinted pool beneath the waterfall. A turtle softly broke the surface, plash, and stared at us curiously as we filed past. Wiskey approached the waterfall to fill his canteen. He peered through discovering a cave.

C-More ordered a perimeter set up while he and I and Stricklyn passed through the cave entrance. Multi-colored light, diffused through the waterfall, danced around the interior and dimly illuminated a fairly large limestone cavern. I crouched in the center adjusting to the change in light, the smell of gooks destroying the serenity.

Look here, said C-More, moving to the corner nearest the entrance, where five large stacked wooden crates had caught his attention. The crates were empty but clearly marked. They were US Care packages addressed to Hanoi. I stared in disbelief as the significance of the mailing labels registered within my limited organic computer.

Wow! Fuck this green motherfucker! is all I could think to say. We're killing and feeding 'em at the same time, dropping bombs on their heads and goodies at their feet.

Ain't this the shits? said Stricklyn, when Raven came in to stare at the discovery. We all laughed as his boyish grin, a grin that stayed there most of the time I knew him, spread wider, curling to one side. EAT THE APPLE – FUCK THE CORPS, he yelled, and we left it at that, the echo reverberating around us.

-31-

And Captain Kody said Let there be a skivvy house.
And there was a skivvy house.
And the Captain said Let business be boom boom.
And business was boom boom.
And the Captain said Let all my men be satisfied.
And all his men were satisfied.

Well, almost all. Some of us didn't mind seconds – thirds even – but my god, there's 140 men in a company and the splib dudes all squeezed to the front of the line.

-32-

SADDLE UP DAMMIT! C-More repeated. We be beatin' feet fast. Captain jus radioed, said recon reported bookoo VC this area. He want us to be regroupin' with 3rd squad, says he's sending 1st platoon out soon's he can. They sposed to sweep, then we mop up behind 'em.

C-More was irritated 'cause we'd already been humpin' over four hours. Now we'd have two hours back to base, an hour of fuckin' around, then two hours back again. The mood of the whole squad changed with the news. Even the climate turned different.

The wind picked up and started blowin' real hard.

I was deep in thought, walkin' along thinkin' about Benjie, comparin' him to high school and all my friends, thinkin' about how close we'd been, how we'd stuck by one another. Thinkin' about the promises we'd made about visiting each other when I got home in the fall, and maybe even livin' together. I moved slowly, stiffly. Benjie was in front of me, his rifle up on his shoulder, butt toward me, one black hand holdin' the flash suppressor, his other swattin' at mosquitos. His bare ass hung out a gaping tear in the back of his filthy trousers. I started to say something, to make a crack, but he beat me to it.

Hey bro, he said, flingin' me a smiling carefree look back over his rifled shoulder. What's hapnin' man? Why yo face be lookin' so low?

You be gone home in twelve days, Benjie. I'm gonna miss you, man. Don't know can I make it without you.

No big thang, he said expressively. We both be gittin' back home. The real world be plenty big for two bad dudes like us.

Guess I'm just worried, Benjie. You been my lookout, man, my partner. I owe you my life.

Be cool Rootie, he said. Don't do nuttin stupid, yo time be up no time. You be home hot on my ass. Sides Rootie, he said, C-More be round help you out.

Suddenly C-More dropped, signaling Quiet, waving us to our knees. The wind picked up bad, blowing worse than I'd ever seen it. There was a village up ahead. I could smell smoke, burning leaves and wet wood. And then the wind changed into gusting, low, sickening moans and came roaring at us slanting rain from the northeast. Lightning pounced and struck the daylight like angry warring laser beams. Crystal cracking strokes of thunder pierced and split the atmosphere. Ozone mixed with the smell of smoke as the rain unexpectedly died to a trickle and the wind gathered more force.

I remember keying on Benjie, watching his stretched eyes and his black face slightly twitchin' like he'd sensed somethin' didn't set right with him. His nose began to flare and I listened hard then, straining outward from the inside. Just as everything went into slow motion, the smell of betel juice filled the air and things started goin' down fast. First – scraping and shuffling. Then – thudthudthud as everyone pitched forward and rolled.

BOOMBOOMBOOM!!! went all three satchel charges damn near at once as Benjie suddenly rose straight up in the air legs first. Stunned from the concussion, I scrambled awkwardly trying to get there to get under him but he came back down on top of his shoulders, both legs sorta crumblin' on his chest and crotch, then flopping off to one side all twisted and contorted, his rifle smackin' his face hard. I froze for a second or two, then sped toward him again, taking his hand gently in mine.

This isn't real, I thought. This can't be happening. Benjie's legs were slabs of tenderized raw flesh, both trouser legs ripped to shreds of individual strips flapping in the wailing wind, slapping at what remained of his legs, lapping up the blood and flinging it in a rectangular pattern. Jagged splintered white bone stood out against the red background. Flies buzzed around the blood. A machine gun tore open a fallen tree trunk to our front. Tracers pierced the dusky sunlight, crissing and crossing like wolves eyes stalking a campfire perimeter.

C-More screamed CHARGE suddenly and the whole squad moved out quickly, zigging and zagging and diving in holes and behind trees, spraying the area like fire fighters, chunks of lead and M-79 rounds exploding on impact. I leapt up too, then fell back down, jerked by Benjie's tight hand on my arm. I looked at his swollen face, watched it turn ashen and then bluish purple as he held his breath fighting the pain and the inevitable, his whole head bloating out, then caving in quickly as his breath rushed out loud.

Rootie, he whispered hoarsely, his fingers gouging deep in my wrist. I be messed up bad, man. Looks... looks like I no be hangin' round... dees lass twelve days.

I looked at him not knowin' what to say. GOD! I remember shouting through clenched teeth. YOU SON-OF-A-BITCH. But God is boys, and I was a boy and couldn't do nothin'. Tears shot out my eyes I remember, rocking back on my heels looking straight up. Arrrrrrrr...... I clenched and screamed, but the wind swept the sounds to the mere decibels of silence.

Dear Me,   24 May 67

So you finally read an article on the 26th Marines. I didn't think anybody knew we were out here. We're always out in the boon docks somewhere. That was us you read about, but the casualty list was much greater than two dead and eighty wounded. One of the boys who died was Benjie, my best friend I've told you about so often. He only had twelve days to go. We may be losing men but the V.C. lose at least four to every one of ours. It's not worth it to me but the big wigs play with statistics.

By the way, please don't throw that party for me when I get home. You know I'll be all embarrassed. After all I don't know your friends anymore. What I mean is – I know who they are but I don't really know them anymore. If you throw a party, everybody's gonna ask me questions about this place and I don't want to talk about it. I hate it and everything about it, so I'd just as soon forget it as soon as possible.

You can ask me, though, cause I can talk to you and make you understand. In fact, in your last letter I think I remember you asking me about the Vietnamese people. Well, there's so many things I could tell you that I'd just as soon not take the time. Maybe when I get home..... Well, I'll tell you one thing. There ain't a one of them I trust. Not a one. Especially including the women and children. And if you're wondering whether I've ever killed any of them – yes I have. I feel sorry in a way, but I'm not exactly ashamed because in my eyes they were all V.C. I don't think I've ever talked to you about it before, but I think that you can probably understand what I'm saying. It's some sort of funny feeling that comes over you when one of your buddies gets hurt. It tends to knot up inside you and make you want to kill anything in sight. Kind of like revenge I guess.

Kind of like last March 15th when Benjie got killed. We received fire from a village, and the order came down over the radio: Kill all the people and burn the homes and crops. I slid quietly but quickly through a hooch back door. An elderly man was sitting at a table. A pregnant woman was working by a hearth. Her daughter stood beside her in a bright red pajama blouse leaning against the rough black stone fireplace. Nobody noticed me at first. I didn't want to do it but something kept saying shoot, shoot, and then the man sensed my presence and I shot and he flew out of his chair and slammed into a corner all twisted up. Then his wife came running at me yelling. She reached for a knife-like tool and kept yelling – I pulled the trigger on automatic point blank. She flew and tumbled across the room. Then this two-year-old little girl just stood there staring at me and screaming. I couldn't stand it but she kept on and on. Screaming and screaming. I couldn't do it but something kept saying – it's an order, it's an order, and Benjie's face kept getting in the way and....I shot. I don't even remember pulling the trigger but suddenly she exploded against the wall and the screaming stopped. I wanted to cry, there was so much blood. It was as though all the bad in all the world had suddenly swept into that home and destroyed it forever. My ears were ringing so bad I turned and ran. I ran darting and zigzagging and screaming and crying and firing my rifle and lobbing grenades. Sometimes at night I can still hear that little girl, see her frightened face. I'll never forget it as long as I live. It was horrible, horrible.

And then people wonder why we want to come home. I want to leave and forget this country ever existed. And when you hear the boys back home bragging about how rough they had it, those are the ones who had it knocked over here. The office pinkies, mail orderlies, truck drivers and mechanics. They're the braggarts. You'll never hear a grunt bragging unless he saw very little action. The Army, the Navy, the Air Force – always bragging and taking home their little souvenirs. It makes me mad, I tell you. The whole thing just tears me up. Sometimes I get so scared I don't think I'll ever make it home. But then most times I just say to hell with it all. I don't give a damn one way or another.

Anyway, don't throw me no parties. I've said my piece already. Said too much I think. Be good.

Love, Rock

P.S. How do you put up with me?

-34-

What the fuck's the problem, Malcolm? You been avoiding me ever since last week.

Nuttin, he practically whispered.

Oh bullshit, don't tell me nothing. We been together too long, been through too much. Shit man we's blood brothers, you forgot?

His eyes looked everywhere but at mine. His head hung low. His right foot shuffled. His hands fiddled around in his pockets. We can't be partners no mo, he said out the corner of his mouth like he didn't want anyone else to hear.

Come on, man, this is me – Rootie – what's going on?

Too much shit gone on man, he answered. All my bros say I can't be hanging out no white dudes no mo, can't be talking like no honkie neither. They say we shouldn't be fightin' no white man's war, shouldn't be killin' minorities when we brothers got no rights our own selves.

I shook my head in disgust. So that's it. You're gonna throw away all we been to each other, a year of friendship. Shit man, we fought together, shed tears together; we slit our fuckin' arms and swore lifetime brotherhood, remember? We burned shitters together, man, took turns with the same women even; we been through pure fuckin' hell and you're not man enough to rise above bullshit peer pressure? Give me a break, Jack. I've called you nigger to your face, remember? You've called me wop, and greaseball. You gonna let that kinda shit split us now? After all that? You know damn well I'd take on any one of these white motherfuckers for you. Remember Phu Bai, man? Remember them five truck drivers calling you a fuckin' nigger, and me lightin' into 'em before you even had a chance to be offended?

He started bobbing, no longer really hearing me. I knew Malcolm like I knew myself. I knew it was time to shut up. He cut me a hateful glance, never really making eye contact, then turned and walked off. I shuffled toward my bunk passing Tony Stagliano on the way. Come on Tony, I demanded, come help me get drunk.

-35-

Dear Me,   4 May 67

Sometimes when I'm drunk I get silly; sometimes I get moody; sometimes sick; sometimes happy; sometimes careless; sometimes intellectual. Sometimes I drink to forget things. Tonight I'm drinking to forget something and at the same time to understand something. I can't forget in order to understand, but then again I can't understand no matter how much I remember. You probably don't know what I'm talking about but I do, so maybe in reality I'm writing to myself in order to better comprehend, but sometimes I consider you a part of me (don't ask me to explain) so I'll address this to New York rather than Vietnam.

Once again I'm faced with a hypothetical question which everyone tries to answer; which no one can. Once again I question God or my creators. Once again I question His way of choosing. It must have been mankind's childhood belief that the good were praised and the bad were punished.

Lance Corporal Charles W. Stricklyn was a good man. He knew not the meaning of bad. He was always good. He would always be good. I know the words all too well. I was taught the meaning of bad. Still I practice it. To be bad is the only way to get ahead in the Corps. In this country to steal is the only way to get clothes on your back, boots on your feet, food in your belly. To kill is the only way to live; to beat is the only way to make some turd listen. Stricklyn was one of few who didn't believe in this. He used charm, understanding and a ready smile to gain his way. He reminded me of Matt – no enemies, only friends. He was a good man; he was to make corporal this month. The lieutenant loved him. He was one of my most intimate friends. He didn't even have to go out this

91

time. But he broke all the cardinal rules and pushed fate. He was wounded in the wrist last week and could have stayed back this time. But noooo. He had to go, he said. He had to be there in case anything happened. Well it did happen, damn it, it did happen.

Charles Stricklyn is dead. With him are Watson, Wiskey, and Murphy. Everyone asks "Why Rizzuti? Someone upstairs must like him. But why him?" I don't know why but I've got to know. Something's got to tell me. I say something cause nothing human can tell me. The guys all think I lead some kind of charmed life. They hang around me like I'm a lucky piece, a Saint Christopher medal or something. Can you believe that? People are dying all around me, and these dudes think I'm lucky.

It's raining outside this leaky tent; artillery is firing and enemy mortar rounds are splashing in the mud. Why don't I take cover? Cause I don't give a damn. I don't give a damn about anything. It just don't mean nothin' no more.

A record player on the other side of this medical ward is spitting out soul music. Most everyone is asleep – some in the bunkers (those that can get up) the rest in their racks. My eyes are drowsy. Soon I'll be blowing eyes with the others.

In about a week you'll probably tear open the closure around these mixed up words. When you've read the words, burn the paper they're placed on. Like I said they were more or less written to me, but only a fool would write to himself – only a fool am I.

I've often told you how I feel about you but I'm not going to tell you anymore. Sometimes you say and do things that piss me off. Mostly you make me happy. I won't distinguish which do which. You're a big girl now. But then I don't guess you much care do you? You have some sort of inner fear to express inner feelings. I never told you this but there have been many nights when I've lain out in ambush under the moon and stars and said to myself "I think I'll ask Me if she wants to get married."

I've said that several times but I don't guess I ever will ask.

There are many reasons involved and I won't go into them because you know them as well, if not better, than I. Anyway, I see some truth in what I'm saying but more than likely I'm wrong in saying it. I think we've been apart too long to know what each one of us is really like. I know the old Me – and I know her only with the old Rock. I have only a dim view of the older, more mature Me just as I have only a dim view of the older, possibly more mature Rock. With all foolishness aside, though, I hope this letter finds you well.

Love, Rock

-36-

When you walk through a storm,
Hold your head up high,
And don't be afraid of the dark.
Walk on in the wind,
Walk on in the rain,
And you'll never walk alone.
You'll never walk alone.

Why you always be singin' dat? asked Watson.

It's kind of like the 23rd Psalm, I answered.

You always singin' or hummin' or whistlin' something'. How come? You got such a terrible voice, you think you'd keep yo mouth shut. Sides, what if some gook hear you, blow yo brains out?

Watson, I said, I think I'd rather go down singin'. It's like my grandmother used to say,

"Canta che ti passa, sing and let it blow over." This ain't exactly no John Wayne movie here. No happy ending coming outa this shit. We gotta create our own happiness here. We gotta find our own beauty. Nothing we've been taught prepared us for this. Man, do you realize we're creating our own reality as we go along? That's pretty scary if you ask me. I always thought our parents did that for us.

93

Aw come on man, said Watson, nobody be doin' my thinkin' long time now.

Watson was from L.A. He was simple and strong. For sheer strength, there was no match in the whole company. He could hump for hours, in full dress gear, four or five bandoliers strung around him, one or two metal boxes of machine gun ammo in one or both hands. If wounded or dead needed carrying, Watson was a mule. I can still hear him moaning Momma over and over. I'll bet when whatever it was that blew us apart exploded, and he was split and fileted open from his chest to his crotch, his mother felt the pain in Los Angeles. The first thing I remember thinking when I looked at him was that I was glad it wasn't me. The guilt resulting from that single thought, however, often made me later wish it had been.

> Dear God above so way up high,
> Sense my anguish, Hear my cry.
> As Watson here no more can waken,
> I pray my brother's soul be taken.

-37-

I remember going to see C-More one day. They had put him on profile and transferred him to third platoon. He was assigned light duty, mess duty actually, what with his bum hand and all. I needed some serious advice, and C-More was the only person I respected enough to seek advice from. We met just outside his barracks. Malcolm and Raven stood rappin' together with someone I didn't know some distance down and across the dusty alleyway separating the long rows of Quonset huts, the exaggerated body languages of all three jukin' an' jivin' in unison. I stuck two dirty fingers in my mouth, let out a shrill whistle and waved at them. They both waved back. C-More's new utilities contrasted starkly with mine, which were torn and covered with old mud, dried blood, gun oil and white salt stains. He seemed self-conscious of the difference so I didn't bring it up.

I can't do it, C-More, I said. What if the rumor's true? What if it really was Murphy's stupidity that got us blowed up? I can't accept a purple heart for that. He was in my fireteam, man. And what about Watson? He was in my fireteam, too. They were my responsibility. I shoulda made them move away when it got light.

Use your head, Rootie, he said. Either way you look at it, Murphy's stupidity got you blowed up. Hell, he was a fuckin' new guy. And dammit, Watson knew better, man; he'd been here four months. He shoulda been paying attention to you, watchin' an learnin'. Sides, two more hearts and you go home, dude, Statesside, FREE-DUMB.

Since I'd considered none of these points, I stood in that award ceremony in stifling heat at attention and, as some general stuck a purple heart pin in my thrustout chest, I flinched but didn't yell, smirked but only C-More saw me, his gold tooth flashing like Morse code, his head twitching in anticipation, his smile big to one side. Good ol' C-More, I thought, always there.

-38-

Impenetrable growth lined both sides of the narrow muddy run-off trail threading its way up the razorback mountain ridge angling toward the summit of Hill 602. We stopped in our tracks to rest and to listen. Somewhere below and to the left, a small tuft-headed gray-white bird warbled its song softly out across the burgeoning tree-top expanse. A large spider monkey shot off a branch, swung to a nearby limb, perched momentarily and chattered in different voices like two excited elderly citizens each trying to get a word in edgewise, then leaped once again, swinging swiftly downward out of sight, scurrying around a gnarled vine-wrapped tree trunk.

The undergrowth, an enmeshed carpet of twisted tangled vines, ferns, lateral shoots and exposed roots, limited our ground view to within a twenty-foot radius. It was late fall – early winter, the smell of molded green life meshing confusedly with the stagnant odors of its own dead and still-living floral ancestry. Gigantic thick rubbery-textured toadstools mushroomed wide across rotted fallen trunks and moss-covered spongy truck-garden black earthen mounds. Deep-treaded, wide-track bark capped huge, towering, deciduous trees that spiraled straight up in the drizzling sky some thirty or forty feet, poking vein-shaped holes in the low-lying cloud cover. Lush, luxuriant boulder ferns fanned outward and away like dozens of bright green turbo props. Effervescent lichen-covered deadwood and exposed knotty roots and runners intermingled equally among folious hardwoods and confused intricate webworks of matted shrubland. This was jungle country – everywhere the same yet nowhere alike – beauty beyond which I'd never beheld, denseness within which I'd never ventured. Fear and pleasure in tug-of-war for my senses, raveled complex patterns defying my abilities to comprehend and define.

Then everything spoke of silence, suddenly: The rain ceased. The fog lifted rapidly under the exhaust control system of an early afternoon sun firing piercing heat rays straight downward. Shafts of light dancing off beads of leaf-trapped water provided glittering showcases of florescent beauty rapidly evaporating before our eyes. No one said a word. No one moved. Bird and insect life came to a complete halt.

Just as suddenly, the sun broke forth in full force, bearing down upon us as one gentle rolling heatwave, like a blast furnace door unexpectedly blown open. We moved onward and upward, slowly and consistently plodding forth, lifting and pushing first one foot forward then the other into thicker steaming vegetation, seeking higher ground and the relief of a breeze.

We stopped again, exhausted from the too moist and heated air. Our squad (second squad) walked company point, Baker leading the way. Take five, said Captain Kody somewhere behind us. I fell down backward against my pack and lit a cigarette, sucking thick smoke deep into already moisture-laden lungs, then coughed up a glob of tart tobacco-tasting phlegm and lobbed it accurately at a slow, snot-trailing slug inching across a nearby log.

Looks like something straight out of Pearl S. Buck, said Malcolm gazing out across jungle expanse.

Who the fuck... is Pearl S. Buck? asked Watson rather rhythmically.

We all laughed.

Take five, expect three, get one! bitched Shorty struggling out of his pack.

Keep the noise down, C-More warned, shaving his K-bar across a leech on his leg. Damn! he swore. Fuckin' cocksucker be thicker'n my thumb.

Another day another dollar, laughed Bobby, flicking a Japanese Beetle off his knee, smacking it up against his rifle.

What's that smell? I asked.

Which one? said C-More.

I'm not sure, I answered. Smells sorta bittersweet – like that juice drooling down the gooks' chins, staining their teeth.

The betel juice, said C-More. You be talkin' bout betel juice.

Suddenly a burp gun shattered the stillness and Baker's jaw. A scream gurgled from deep within his throat. I froze unable to move, petrified in place.

POINT MAN DOWN! shouted someone.

CORPSMAN! CORPSMAN! rose the cry coupled with frantic, scurrying confusion. I struggled to rise, to move off the trail, but my legs refused to obey.

SMOKE'S DOWN! someone screamed.

SO'S GEORGE! yelled someone else.

THEY'RE DEAD, MAN! THEY'RE DEAD!

GUNS UP! GUNS UP! shouted Captain Kody. Get them guns to the front, he ordered as Wiskey and Stricklyn wound their way forward, crouched low, their eyes stretched taut, their breathing heavy and rapid as they worked up the path, over and around me, hundred-round bandoliers of 7.62 mm machine gun ammo swinging inches by my face.

RIZZUTI! snapped Lieutenant Birch. TAKE POINT!

Point? I thought. Point? No, man, I just got here. I'm too young to die. CRACKATA CRACKATA... CRACKATA CRACKATA... CRACKATA CRACKATA CRACKATA barked the smoking M-60. Our Father... Our Father. I struggled for the words, my hand riffling through the motions of the sign of the cross, over and over and over again.

RIZZUTI!

I cringed, terrorstruck and immobile, frozen in place.

GET YOUR ASS UP ON POINT!

Our Father... Oh God... I am heartily sorry... I've forgotten my... my catechism... my lessons.

RIZZUTI!

Yesss... ssir, I stammered, rising slowly, my legs dead, skin crawling, hair tingling and standing on end, my whole body wobbling spasmodically, icy fingers of dread raking gooseflesh in their wake.

I moved toward the front, one step at a time, slowly past staring eyes as frightened as my own, then froze solid again as Baker's and mine locked in instantaneous telepathy. I looked away quickly, but not before registering one life-lasting color photo of his mutilated face, torn off from the nose down, shredded flesh oozing blood and saliva, dripping like melting cherry icicles, splattering off his flak jacket and boots, his eyes wild and glossy like someone speaking in tongues, his arms and shoulders limp, his hands wringing frantically at rosary beads, his sunken life's essence hurling toward total completion – He knew it – I knew it – God knew it – everyone and everything abandoning him on this, the afternoon of his supreme and inevitable day.

I rushed past him with renewed strength. No gook's gonna do that to me, I swore, zaggin' and ziggin' side to side, tree to tree, rock to rock, hittin' the deck gun-butt first, rolling and rebounding back up, crouched low, charging fast now, Bobby hot on my ass, both of us growling... arrrrrrrrrrr... when suddenly the automatic opened up again, a four or five round blast that ripped up the dead-wood on my right as I dove left through the vines, rolled, came back up firing, and Bobby dove too, catching a round head-on with his kneecap, the snap resounding as the subsequent cracks of the crashing trees beneath the supporting artillery rounds whooshing in over our heads from the rear.

I buried my face in the damp musty leaves and mud, eye-to-eye with a milk-white earth grub, recalling the shouts of FIRE IN THE HOLE signaling the summoned artillery support, and the ON THE WAY warnings to let us know it was time to dig in and pray the coordinates had been called in correctly and the trajectories ac-curately determined.

Shorty and C-More crawled up to help me guard the trail as

Mack worked on Bobby's shattered knee, blood all over the place, the lower half of his leg twisted 180 degrees, jagged ivory bone protruding out the top of his shin. He was in agony, a world of hurt, shock on his face, wincing and rocking and crying IT HURTS BAD DOC, IT HURTS BAD to Mack who quickly shot him again to put him out of his misery but this time with morphine. Captain Kody was screaming MEDIVAC! GET ME MEDIVAC! to the radio that squelched back It's on the way.

We broke out the C-4 and cleared an LZ, but when the chopper arrived sniper fire broke out and the pilot steered clear. One more rescue was attempted, but the sniper fire intensified and everyone just sorta looked at Bobby and Baker who, recognizing the hopelessness, nevertheless tried to seem optimistic. The Captain ordered Bobby and Baker put on stretchers, and shifts were assigned to carry them down, but Baker shook his head side to side and motioned that he'd walk.

SADDLE UP! MOVE OUT! shouted Kody.

Rizzuti, ordered C-More, take Tail End Charley. Bendix, take Smoke. Carl, grab George. Let's go, move out.

Tail End Charley was just as spooky as Point. You never knew when gooks would attack your rear. And when it got dark, the stress intensified because it was easy to get left behind and lost. We usually moved single file with fifteen or twenty paces between each person. It was a tough distance to maintain because there's safety in numbers and crowds, but the phobia of one round getting us all outweighed the majority of these psychological warfareisms.

It was fast approaching dusk when we moved down off 602. The darker it got the more I relied on Baker's blood drips marking the route. Ten minutes from the bottom, foreboding took hold of me, suddenly, in the form of an odor, a bittersweet odor, the same one I'd mentioned earlier to C-More just before... just before... HIT THE DECK! I screamed as C-More and Shorty and I dove and an AK-47 crack-cracked and recrack-cracked, and Shorty blooped and reblooped his M-79 point blank tearing up the trail behind us ... BLOOP-BOOM ... BLOOP-BOOM ... BLOOP-BOOM .... C-More and I opened up on automatic burping out rounds at no one and nothing in particular, tearing up the silence like two thunderstorms vying for the same space.

Baker stumbled in the valley at the foot of Hill 602 looming behind us. He stumbled again some sixty yards from the hovering chopper waiting to dust him off to medical attention. Captain Kody grabbed one of his arms and Lieutenant Birch took the other as they helped him forward. His rosary broke and he made a spastic stab at it, knocking the beads all over the ground. I watched his legs buckle again and again as he fought toward the outstretched arms of the medical crew hanging out the open door. The chopper was too high as Kody and Birch tried to stretch Baker up who was completely sagging now, near dead weight.

TOUCH DOWN! screamed Kody to the pilot. TOUCH DOWN!

The chopper sank lower and the medics fumbled Baker as they reached forward and grabbed him quickly, each of their faces absorbing the horror in his. No Pulse! I read on the shaking lips of the medic who laid Baker on the floor beside several intermingled dead bodies and covered him with a poncho. Bobby was crying NO! NO! shaking his fist at the chopper pilot who lifted his ship suddenly, tail first, sweeping forward slightly, then sideways before swooping upward and away. I looked at Shorty who looked at me as both of us turning toward 602 said in unison We'll be back, Motherfucker, we'll be back.

-39-

Dear Me,   25 Jan 67

No I didn't get to see the Bob Hope show. Where in hell do you think I am? I'm in a hole, woman, a hole – with rats running around. And I mean that literally too. We go on patrols every other day, sometimes for days, and ambushes on the nights in between. We take baths every two weeks, if we're lucky. I mean we stink – STINK. I smoke like a fiend and drink straight booze and smoke pot whenever we can beg, borrow, steal or buy it from villagers. We walk through shit you wouldn't believe and live like pigs – worse even.

I'm not trying to make you feel sorry for me. On the

contrary, I'm just trying to set you straight on the situation. We don't get to see U.S.O. shows like the pussies in the Army, Navy and Air Force. The only ones in the Marine Corps that go are the mail orderlies, office pinkies and air wing. We're grunts, woman, out in the middle of no where, with a job to do – a job that sucks and shouldn't be asked of anyone. When we're not patrolling we're working – doing this, doing that – petty-assed shit just to keep us going. The staff and officers can't stand to see us resting.

Nearly every letter you get from me is written by candle light at night when I should be getting all the sleep I can. So please understand, when you don't get a letter it's because I'm tired, dead tired. A body can only take so much, and believe me we get pushed pretty hard.

We're north of Da Nang now, on Hill 458, and we hump all our supplies up on our backs – chow, ammo, water, etc. They could bring it in by choppers but the Marine Corps doesn't believe in doing things the easy way. Please take care and for heaven's sake don't ask me no more dumb questions, and don't go getting yourself involved with no other boys neither. Even if they are as good looking as me.

Love, Rock

P.S. Did you ever ask your boss if I could get some free insurance? Could sure use some over here.

-40-

It was November 20, 1967, the day I turned twenty-one. I was standing in my parent's backyard, daydreaming while watching my father plant grass plugs. It seemed late in the year for that, but I didn't say anything. The yard was all red dirt, reminding me of Nam, the house having been built only just recently. It didn't seem like home to me since I'd only lived there about seven days. I began drifting farther and farther from Oklahoma, closer and closer to Nam...

Six-bys lined the red, muddy camp road for a quarter of a mile, ready to thunder run north through the city of Hue toward Cam Lo and the DMZ. There was to be a short supply stop at L.Z. Hardcore. Our truck ran Tail End Charley, which was good because point trucks and the second ones back unwillingly served as mine sweepers, frequently blowing all to hell and back after tripping recently planted land mines.

There were five of us in the sandbag-covered bed and two in the cab when the convoy suddenly lurched forward and began picking up speed like a freight train. I manned the .50 caliber mounted on the roof above the passenger side, a powerful machine gun that had a tendency to transfer its strength into any operator familiar with its potential. Serious trouble could come from anywhere along this treacherous stretch of road just south of Hue; nonetheless, I felt invincible. The wind was blowing strong against my face as I sighted down the length of its long barrel, practicing in my mind how I'd handle an ambush situation.

Sergeant Rotan lay against his pack trying to sleep, his helmet pulled down over his face. An ugly scar squiggled from behind his left ear and disappeared inside his collar. Gun grease and sweat stained his trouser thighs. His shirt tail hung out, and grenades bulged out the bottom pockets. His hands were deeply tanned and covered with black grime and old scabs. His right thumb was dark black and blue. Probably got it slammed on by the bolt while cleaning his rifle. That happened sometimes. His jungle boots, scuffed and scraped bare of the original polish, were covered with the red powdered dust that coated everyone and everything. It was about 1630, and the heat and humidity were unbearable as usual. We were headed north and I was looking forward to passing through Hue again, the old capital of Vietnam. The red brick city streets were always a surprise. And the gorgeous girls strolling two-by-two on the all-female campus were a surprise. And the Shell gas station, the only gas station I ever saw in Nam, was a surprise. And the fantastic architecture was likewise everywhere a surprise.

We slowed then came to a halt, backed up by the bridge ahead. You gimme chop chop? You gimme chop chop? Kids gathered all around reaching for handouts. Sergeant Rotan, moodier than I'd ever seen him before, stood up, dropped his drawers and pissed in a plastic bag full of food stuff; then, while handing it over the tailgate toward a small kid, purposefully dropped it on the ground bursting at his feet.

Ooh, you numbah ten, you numbah fucking ten, said the kid. Sergeant Rotan glared at him, pure hatred in his expression. You numbah fucking ten, the little boy repeated with great emphasis on each word. His sister began pulling at him, recognizing the potential danger I think. Just then the caravan lunged forward and I tried to relax, leaning back against the cab, sighting down the .50 caliber. Slowly I nudged my rifle to my side, undetected by the others, my sixth sense working overtime.

A few miles north of Hue, along the Street Without Joy south of Quanq Tri, we approached an extension bridge out over the Perfume River. Out on one of the railings stood an ARVN hanging out his wash on one of the guy wires. Sergeant Rotan spotted him about the same time I did and grabbed his M-14 by the barrel. Just as we came abreast of the ARVN, Rotan swung his rifle hard, smacking him up side the head and drilling him into the pilings and water some thirty feet below. There was no doubt he had to have been dead on impact. I grabbed my rifle quickly and flicked off the safety, preparing myself for action, but Sergeant Rotan laid back down, a much satisfied expression on his face over which he replaced his helmet.

That's one BAD motherfucker, said Raven.

Yeah buddy, agreed Shorty, his head rockin' up and down.

I pretended to play no part in this particular scene for which an ending had yet been written. Lieutenant Little glared out the cab window at Rotan's outstretched form, his face clenched tight, the skin wrinkled. Morality was a capitol offense to Rotan, we all knew, which is why he set his sights on Little, who despite his inefficiencies, because of the bars he wore represented all that was considered right in the world....

Julie, a dark haired, dark complected nineteen-year-old neighbor suddenly walked up and introduced herself. I nodded as we stood there slightly embarrassed.

You don't look much younger than your father, she pointed out.
Thanks, we both said.

She realized immediately what she'd done and changed the subject quickly. What was it like in Vietnam? she asked. Don't you feel proud? I mean, going to Vietnam and all, and getting to fight Communists. Don't you feel just like a hero?

When I disgustedly responded NO, she pressed for details I was unwilling to provide. I felt like I did at the dinner table my first night home, my family grilling me for information. What was it like? Did you have to kill anyone? What about drugs? You didn't smoke any of that awful marijuana did you? I remember thinking I didn't belong there anymore, with my family I mean. I felt alone again. This was Midwest City, Oklahoma, and I didn't know anyone.

So I drove to Norman, to the University, to look up and visit old friends, but they were all studying hard for finals and didn't have time for me. So I drove to Oklahoma City, to a night club I remembered called the Sword and Stone, but I didn't have any hair and felt out of place. The three girls I asked to dance each turned me down so I decided to drive back to Norman, thinking there had to be something going on there worth doing. After all, it was a University town, and students were supposed to be such activists.

I was traveling I-35 headed south. The speed limit was 70. I'd just executed the S-curve through the town of Moore when the adrenaline hit. I had always enjoyed driving fast, and it had been a long time. I lit a cigarette. The road, I remembered, stretched straight for the next five or six miles. I was in a '64 six-cylinder Chevy Malibu. I eased the throttle to the floor and held it there. Seventy-five, eighty, eighty-five. There was no traffic to speak of, and road conditions couldn't be better. Ninety, ninety-five, a hundred. It felt good, real good. The front end had started to shimmy a little and the scenery was slipping by fast, when suddenly everything popped into slow motion and I felt comfortable for the first time in weeks. A hundred and five. The tires, I laughed, how good are the tires? A hundred and ten. The speedometer vibrated erratically. The car was topped out, and Norman was coming up fast. The front end shook violently. Happy Birthday to me, Happy

Birthday to me. Drive this mother through a wall; fuck the world, I thought, fighting back the tears and the adrenaline, but most of all the boredom. Where was the brass band? Where were all the draft card and bra burners I'd heard about? The country seemed dead. In Nam, even though people were dying the country was alive, very much alive. There was action all the time. The transition was hard for me, as well as for others I would talk to about it later. Fuck it, I thought. Raven and Malcolm will be pissed if I die on a damn highway before they get back. I backed off the accelerator and coasted into Norman. That night I slept fitfully, wondering over and over and over: What was it like in Vietnam – How in hell do you describe it?

Go wake up your brother, my father ordered my nine-year-old brother who ran to my room all excited and jumped on my chest the next morning. I woke and leapt and grabbed him by the throat, growling and wrestling him to the floor. He'd be dead now had my father not quickly reacted to his own mistake, recognizing it for an error none to soon, his own post-war feelings rising from the depths of his repressed experiences. I remember cowering in the corner, staring about the room wondering if I'd ever be able to adjust to myself and my new life. I rose up and took the .45 down out of the closet where I'd hidden it, clutching the security it provided, and squatted back down in the corner on the floor rocking back and forth, knees up under my cheek bones, peeking out over them like Kilroy looking over a wall. I'll be leaving for New York, I later told my parents, as soon as I can arrange a flight. There's some people I want to see.

-41-

Ain't you worried about that .45, Rootie? You gotta go through customs you know. I was worried, but it wasn't about customs inspections. I was worried about hippies and draft card burners; I was worried about riots and students attacking the plane when we landed. All my information in Nam suggested that GIs were on the ten-most-hated list. I literally expected to have to fight my way off the plane. The .45 strapped to my leg only provided marginal insulation against the insecurity I had bottled up inside.

STEWARDESS, someone asked, why are we circling? We should've landed over an hour ago.

Air Force One is landing ahead of us, she said. President Johnson wants to greet each of you personally. Besides, it's very foggy out there. And besides again, today's the Marine Corps birthday, she said, trying to muster up some enthusiasm, to put some life into the party so to speak.

We landed finally and were chatteled into a reception area where each of us was customized and handed our leave papers and next duty assignment. The terminal room was absolutely quiet. No one was talking or even fidgeting or coughing, when an El Toro General announced that all volunteers were to proceed to the parade field. President Johnson was gonna talk to us. A colonel and a sergeant major headed for the parade deck. The General looked us over sternly, all 200 or so of us, and said Am I to understand that none of you wish to greet the President? No one said a word. You, son, stand up! he ordered pointing at me. I rose to a relaxed attention. Don't you want to meet President Johnson? he asked.

No sir, I said.

But why not, son? Don't you realize this may be your lifetime chance to meet a president of the United States?

I thought about the .45 for a second. Then I thought about a letter home I'd written:

Dear Me,   7 Dec 66

Thanks for the card. The ice cream cone on the front made me hungry. You said you'd better get a letter soon and I must say you rate getting one every day, but you see I can't always write that often. I'm going to try to make this one as long as possible though because I'm afraid I won't be able to write for the next four days or so. We have to go out on some silly-assed operation involving our whole battalion. Just what I've been wanting – another chance to get out in the rain amongst all them lovely leeches. That's the way it goes though. We do all the dirty work while our White House handlers sit back and comment on the wonderful job the Marines are doing. You know what I'd like? A five-minute interview with LBJ or his honorable Mr. McNamara. Boy I'd tell them mothers where to go. Ain't I a dreamer though? No way I'll ever get to meet the President.

You just made me so happy and you probably don't even know it. I just now got handed a letter from you. It was so sweet I almost cried. You said you hate to write lonely letters cause they might make me sad. They don't make me sad, they make me happy 'cause I know you're thinking about me the same way I'm thinking about you. Hell I'd give the world to walk you down the street tonight and throw you in a pile of leaves. And if there ain't no leaves I'll pick you up and drop you in a snow bank. You probably think I've forgotten all the good times we've had. Well I haven't. In fact the things I can't seem to remember too well are the times we were fighting. And don't think I've forgotten your birth date either, 'cause I haven't. And I can even still remember when you and a bunch of girls went someplace to stay for a weekend or so and you sent me a real long letter telling me all about it and how you slept with my picture and got it all crumbled up. See? Boys remember things too. They just don't admit it.

The operation just got changed to tonight instead of tomorrow but I can't seem to get depressed like usual. Your letter gave me such a boost. Oh God, I'm sorry but I just got further word that we're moving out in an hour. I wanted to make this much longer but I'm afraid I can't. I won't be able to write for about four days like I said, but I'll be with you anyway. Take care.

Much Love, Rock

No particular reason sir, I answered, just wanna get home.

There it is, said someone behind me. A murmur of agreement spread through the room quickly. The general looked at us as though we were all out of our cotton pickin' minds. He was shaking his head slightly, side to side, in disgusted disbelief. The least you all could do is show some respect for the Marine Corps birthday, he said.

We showed our respect all day yesterday, General, said someone from the rear. Even the Marine Corps don't rate no double birthday, sir.

-42-

Well how about it, son, said the captain, four more years isn't such a very long time. I can get you $5,000 and a new car. Whata you say? Will you stay in? Ship over? You'll be out in 1973. I can also get you the duty station of your choice.

Just hand me my pink ID card, sir. I wanna get on the road, I said, get on with my life.

But sergeant, he said, why? Why do you want out so bad? The Marine Corps' a good life, and we need good NCOs. Think it through for a minute before you answer.

I thought back to the previous morning...

FALL OUT! screamed the captain and we fell out. We're moving out on bivouac in one hour, he shouted. I want every swingin' dick out here ready to march at 0900. DISMISSED!

I walked up to him, saluted and said, I'm getting out tomorrow, sir. I'd appreciate being excluded from this march since all my gear is turned in.

He glared at me with pure hatred written all over his body. Are you deaf, Sergeant? he snapped. Or just plain ignorant? I said every swingin' dick, and when I say every swingin' dick I mean every swingin' dick, unless of course your dick don't swing.

I remember wishing I could get an instant hardon so I could drop my drawers and prove it really didn't swing, but I swallowed hard and thought: BOHICA, I can put up with anything for just one day. It was December 4, 1969, though, and cold in North Carolina. Anyone who's been there knows the hawk is one bad dude in North Carolina come winter. I had no blanket, no poncho, no sleeping bag, no nothing. I stayed awake all night freezing my you know whats off, thinking about the next day and the freedom it'd bring. BOHICA, I thought: Bend Over, Here It Comes Again. Fucked and refucked every time you turn around in this green son-of-a-bitch.

And I thought back three and a half years to bootcamp and Sergeant Roderick, our DI. He slammed me up against the washroom bulkhead, his face growling inches away from mine, his breath hot and tobacco smelly.

Would you fuck my wife, maggot?

Sir, No Sir.

I can't hear you.

SIR! NO SIR!

You wouldn't fuck my wife, maggot?

SIR! NO SIR!

What's a matter, maggot, ain't she good enough for you?

SIR! YES SIR!

OH! So you *would* fuck my wife, huh maggot?

SIR! NO SIR!

Make up your mind, maggot, would you fuck my wife or not?

SIR! NO SIR!

GET DOWN AND GIVE ME FIFTY PUSHUPS FORE I BASH YER BRAINS IN!

SIR! YES SIR! SIR! PRIVATE RIZZUTI REQUESTS PERMISSION TO GET DOWN AND GIVE YOU FIFTY PUSH-UPS SIR!

YOU? YOU? You see any female sheep around here, maggot?

SIR! NO SIR!

GET OUTA MY SIGHT, MAGGOT! YOU SKUMMY FUCKIN' CIVILIAN!

SIR! YES SIR! SIR! PRIVATE RIZZUTI REQUESTS PERMISSION TO GET OUTA SIGHT SIR!

GO, MAGGOT! GO! GO! GO! GO!

And I thought back to Vietnam, to a letter I'd written:

Dear Me,   10 Dec 66

So how's things going out that way? It's too bad about your

friend and her possible case of mono. Remember when Charlie got it? He was layed up for two months. Oh well, at least mono isn't as bad as malaria.

It's funny but I can't seem to keep my mind on what I'm writing. We had a pretty rough go of it the past few days, and three of my buddies died yesterday. One of them was Tommy Baker. You remember me talking about him. They shot his face off. It was bad and I don't feel so good and can't seem to write straight. You know what I mean? The only thing good that came out of yesterday is that now the guys seem to have finally accepted me. I'm no longer a boot around here.

I'm sorry but I'm going to cut this short 'cause I just can't seem to concentrate at the moment. I miss you so much.

Please understand. God, I gotta get outa this place.

Love, Rock

And I thought back to that field dentist in Nam who pulled my tooth without using Novocain:

What's the verdict? I asked him.

I have to remove it, he answered. It's rotten to the core and there's no restoring it.

What about all the others?

They'll need some attention eventually, he said, but let's extract this serious problem first.

I leaned back but remained erect, opened wide to the drill cadence hovering before my face, felt the vibration but smothered the pain. Damn! I swore. Hurts like hell and smells like decayed flesh...

I'd rather not discuss it, sir, I said. Just give me my pink ID card. It's kind of like when you step in a pile of fresh dog shit, sir, you know what I mean? What's the first thing you do when you step in a pile of dog shit? He got an exasperated look on his face as he waited for the answer. Well sir, you get the fuck out of it and you wipe your foot clean. And that's what I'm doing, sir. I'm getting out of this shit now, and I'm gonna clean up my life. He tossed the ID card across his desk toward me. I picked it up, saluted for the last time, about faced for the last time, and headed out the door. Passing through the Camp Lejeune main entrance gate, I remember feeling as though a great burden had been lifted off my chest. I was scared too, admittedly, but it was the exciting kind of fear that accompanies life changes. I smiled from true happiness for the first time in nearly four years.

-43-

I figure we're nearly half way, said C-More, maybe more but I doubt it. Six hundred and two feet is a long uphill battle when you're avoiding trails as much as possible. It was maybe an hour or so before dusk when we stopped in a small clearing on the edge by a stream trickle. Resting on top of a small boulder was a skull. I didn't see it at first. When I recognized what it was I instinctively shuddered, wondering how old it could be. It looked fairly clean but smelled slightly and had a few tiny ants roaming around one of the eye sockets. Someone said Hamlet when I held it up, vis a vis, puckering my lips in a mock kiss.

Ever notice how skulls all look alike to the untrained eye, even across ethnic groups? asked Malcolm.

Watson whispered Let's get outa here, man, it's spooky.

C-More was nervous, fidgeting with his sling. No sound escaped the clearing as though, straining as we were, our ears soaked up each and every decibel like sponges, not daring to let them carry beyond range of the circling trees. Suddenly Raven held up another skull he'd found a few feet away. Then, as though our eyes had developed greater discriminating vision, skulls turned up everywhere we looked. No other bones were anywhere else to be found. Only skulls. Forty-three of them altogether. Fear swept over us like a witch's broom. An owl hooted, softly at first, then louder and with more frequency, each series of WHO, WHO sounding as though it was emitted from a different location, but always in the vicinity of one of the skulls. It was as though that owl had ventriloquial powers. Watson's eyes got big and bright like silver dollars. So did Stricklyn's.

What happened here? he asked.

111

Who knows, answered Watson.

I replaced the skull I'd been holding exactly as I'd found it. Then, as if on cue, we each prepared to move out. A snap sounded from across the clearing, though, and everyone froze. HALT....who goes there? called C-More too softly. WHO, WHO repeated the owl just before fluttering swiftly from one branch to another. We ran and ran, crashing upward in reckless abandon, no precaution whatsoever until, again as though on cue, we finally threw ourselves upon the ground in one huge clashing ball of total exhaustion.

When we recovered, a snake slithered past my face in the Japanese evergreen I was leaning against. When it stopped I moved, and when it moved I stopped. This snake was unlike any I'd ever seen before or since. It wasn't a rattlesnake; I was sure of that. It might have been a bamboo snake. It was short, maybe a foot and a half long, but looked full grown. It was well camouflaged, light and dark greenish brown, knotty skin like the trees it inhabited, bright slanted black pupiled eyes, triangular pointed head with short horns sloping outward from each of the upper corners.

I stuck my K-Bar toward its flicky-tongued face. It reared rapidly and struck in one swift flash of motion, then recoiled and struck again, each time hissing and spewing venom across the tip of my K-Bar. Instinctively I drew back, sensing I was in real danger. Most snakes will slither off. But this one held its ground. Get out of my way, it seemed to say. I teased it again, and again it struck and restruck, emitting a strange cracking sound as it did so. One more time I teased it. This time, as though staging its final assault, it reared up practically on its tail and took a tremendous strike forward, completely losing its balance and flipping out of the tree onto the ground at my feet. I leaped out of its way, but not before it had recovered and struck again catching my jungle boot top. Again it held its ground. Torn between killing it and leaving it alone, I moved on thinking anything that determined deserved both peace and respect.

-44-

It was May 1967. We sat in a stoned circle passing a joint laced with local heroin while Frank, the corpsman, was trying to clean his loaded .45 automatic. It went off blowing a neat little hole in Wagner's foot, spinning his leg around and him off the cot. We laughed and laughed, aware of the ludicrousness of the situation yet unable to stop. Wagner was rolling on the floor in a totally uncontrollable fit of laughter, his foot in his hands in the air bleeding all over himself.

CORPSMAN! CORPSMAN! shouted Frank just as Lieutenant Little burst through the door, a strained look on his face that instantly turned white. CORPSMAN! shouted Frank one more time.

What the hell's going on? Little asked quizzically, you're the duty corpsman.

Oh yeah, squeaked Frank looking around and grabbing the dope bag instead of his medical pack. We laughed and laughed, our hands covering our mouths, but Little didn't think it was funny.

Lucky for Frank and the rest of us, though, Sergeant Rotan shot Lieutenant Little in the leg two nights later before he'd had a chance to initiate court-martial proceedings. Since Rotan hated Little's guts so much, he decided to spill some by marching him at gun point out past the wire, where he could say he thought it was a gook. He even brought along one of those gook conical hats to make it look more convincing. He was gonna lay it upside the body, he said later, maybe cover his face with it so nobody'd have to look at his ugly mug.

Lieutenant Little was so scared shitless he figured his only chance was to make a break for it, so he dove around the front of a jeep to make a getaway. Rotan emptied a whole twenty-round magazine at him, and managed to put two bullets in his lower leg, shattering the shin bone. We never saw Rotan or Little again. Supposedly they roared Little's assailant off to LBJ, Long Binh Jail, but rumor had it they stuck him in Special Forces or Recon where his kind seemed to thrive. Little, we were told, lost his leg and got flown out to Japan for rehabilitation.

What did you say, Raven? I asked.

It don't mean nothin', he answered, not a damn fuckin' thing.

-45-

Rice paddies formed vast interwoven networks of English and Chinese checkerboards, like huge boxes of assorted chocolates, each individually wrapped in long, narrow, earthen, geometrically shaped dikes which, when trod upon by platoon- or company-size patrols, reduced to just so much sunken sludge. No sooner had a dozen or two troopers crossed any particular dike when those following in their footsteps found themselves trudging through nasty, smelly cesspools of leech infested water.

Gooks sensed American squeamishness, often opening fire at the most vulnerable of times, sending gear-burdened troops thrashing through open rice paddy terrain in search of scarce, but "suitable," cover. Sometimes it was hard to decide whether flagrant risk was a worse fate than endless reclining in leech-infested, buffalo-shitty, rice paddy water while cowering behind foot high mud dikes. Like the time when we got pinned down northwest of Phu Loc smack in the center of a two-square mile rice paddy acreage.

It had certainly seemed secure enough to cross in the wide open. After all, families of farmers clad in black could be seen through-out the area, planting and weeding in their normal everyday bent, bobbing way, seemingly oblivious of our presence, their true ex-pressions hidden beneath conical straw hats. But then Walter Singleton took a round in the left shoulder that sent him plunging backward tripping over a knee-high dike flat on his blindside. Within seconds, 82 mm mortar rounds came roaring in all sudden like – whoowhooshwhoosh, booboomboom – whoowhoosh whoosh, booboomboom. I buried my head in the pukiest slop I've ever tasted.

CORPSMAN! screamed C-More.

HE'S DOWN, MAN, DEAD! shouted back Raven to C-More who ordered Ronald (a brand-spanking new guy that very day) to check out Walter's wound, which wasn't all that serious, although for Walter everything in the whole world was serious, particularly his love life, if you can call no love life a love life that is.

Walter was one of those rare individuals caught up in a world totally alien to his life style. Twenty-six years old, he had meant to join the Navy straight out of a five-year pharmacy-school program at the University of Rhode Island. He entered the wrong line, however, while undergoing his physical examination preceding military induction, and as providence would have it, mistakenly joined the Marine Corps. We'd been razzin' him for nearly two months about his never having had a piece of ass.

I beg your pardon, he had said. How dare you insinuate I'd stoop to such revolting behavior.

Revotin' behavior no stop yo momma, said Watson.

Walter was about as pissed as I'd ever seen him, although intelligent enough to recognize not only the wisdom behind Watson's statement but also the fact that his mother's honor and his own pride weren't worth dying over.

Mortars were dropping in like old home week. They blew humpback-sized waterspouts, slapped the mud like furious crocodiles. MOVE OUT! screamed C-More. MOVE OUT! GO-GO-GO! he yelled. Watson grabbed Walter by his uninjured arm, yankin' him up in a fireman's carry as we all made a bee-line away from the mortars. Everyone was runnin' and jumpin' and stumblin' and fallin' when suddenly Murphy and Wiskey went down in a sinkhole then popped back up thrashing wildly. Stricklyn threw his M-60 down in the mud, squirmed out of his backpack at a dead run, and lunged into the sinkhole. Murphy grabbed hold of him, pulling him under in panic. Wiskey, struggling all around trying to get his bandoliers off, finally got out of there. C-More was blowing frantically on a rubber lady to provide a buoy, hyperventilating himself into another world. The mortars had been recalculated, exploding waterspouts walking toward us at an alarming pace. Watson dropped Walter like a hot spud, lumbering his way to provide assistance. Raven was studying the maps trying to pinpoint the mortar site while I worked the radio requesting artillery support.

115

GOLF 4 THIS IS GOLF 2, OVER! GOLF 4 THIS IS GOLF 2, OVER! GOLF 4, GOLF 4 THIS IS GOLF 2, GOLF 2. DO YOU READ ME, OVER?

This is GOLF 4, GOLF 2. Read you loud and clear, over.

GOLF 4 THIS IS GOLF 2. BLOW THE HELL OUT THE EAST SIDE OF HILL 442 ABOUT TWO-THIRDS UP, OVER.

This is GOLF 4, GOLF 2. Say again, over.

GODDAMMIT GOLF 4! BLOW THE HELL OUT OF HILL 442 ABOUT TWO-THIRDS UP THE EAST SIDE, OVER.

What's the coordinates GOLF 2?

YOU DEAF MAN! AIN'T NO TIME FOR COORDINATES. WE GOT PEOPLE DOWN. BLOW THE WHOLE DAMN HILL AWAY, OVER.

Gimme dat sum-bitch, demanded Raven grabbing the handset out of my hand and screaming into it – JAKE! JAKE! THIS IS RAVEN GODDAMMIT. YOU GOT TWO FUCKIN SECONDS BLOW 442 AWAY!!

GOLF 2, GOLF 2, EXECUTE PROPER RADIO USAGE, OVER.

ONE! screamed Raven. TWO! Jake's a dead dude, Raven said to me, his thumb pressing the talk button.

FIRE IN THE HOLE! yelled the radio.

ON THE WAY! Raven shouted.

Within seconds came the boomboombooms, boomboombooms, followed by the whistling swooshes preceding the bambambams slammin' up against the east side of Hill 442. The mortars quieted immediately. I turned toward Watson who was draggin' Murphy and Stricklyn out of the sinkhole by their collars, a big shit-eatin' grin spread across his flat face. Wiskey and C-More just stood there shaking their heads incredulously.

Then, while looking out across the corpsman's dead body and the vast paddy network, I realized the farmers had all gone about business as usual in a kind of stoic denial of the dangerousness of the situation, almost as though nothing was even happening, as if to say that Since this is not our war, by simply ignoring it it will cease to exist. Soon, amazingly, I would develop similar survival techniques.

What do you mean we're trading our M-14s in for M-16s? Ours was the bastard battalion, so we caught all the shit details. Two twenty-six was part of the 5th Marine Division, only the 5th Marines weren't stationed in Nam yet. They were still states-side. So 2/26 was temporarily attached to the 3rd Marine Division which was in Nam, and even sometimes loaned out to the 1st. Whenever a particularly nasty or dangerous situation came up, the task fell to 2/26. This time we were to be the first Marines in Nam to test the new M-16s. That's like giving someone a brand new Corvette for off-road racing. To make a long story short, several of our people died and hundreds more were wounded simply because we switched rifles in mid-war. BOHICA.

The M-14 rifle is as rugged and powerful as a tank. It fires 7.62 mm rounds that are about three inches long. A fully loaded twenty-round magazine weighs nearly two pounds. We usually carried as many as we could fit on a cartridge belt, up to eleven if you didn't carry water. Some guys needed more water than others, carrying three or four canteens. I carried two canteens of water (about four or five pounds), a first aid kit and five to seven magazines on my cartridge belt. I also carried one magazine in my flak jacket pocket and another taped upside down to the one in my rifle. An M-14 rifle with bipods and two magazines weighed in at about eighteen pounds. It was heavy and bulky but could be taken anywhere under any adverse conditions and it always worked.

The M-16 rifle is light and versatile. It fires 5.56 mm rounds that are about twice the size of .22 caliber longs. M-16 rifles, magazines and rounds weighed about half their M-14 counterparts. The M-16 is more sophisticated, more sensitive like a fine tuned sports car, requiring frequent preventive maintenance if it's to be trusted. Where mud, sand and rust would literally jump off an M-14 as soon as its trigger was pulled, these same agents converted M-16s into useless muzzle loading single-shots. Frightened troops could frequently be seen scattered throughout a fire zone frantically slamming cleaning rods down barrels trying to clear jammed chambers.

Gooks carried any weapon they could put their hands on. They seemed to favor carbines and AK-47s, Russian made assault rifles. Carbines weren't that effective, but AK-47s were very useful, about midway between M-14s and M-16s. They also carried 61 mm and 82 mm mortar units, as opposed to our 60s and 81s. Everything they had was a millimeter larger. That meant they could fire our ammo but we couldn't use theirs.

Except for the cumbersome RPG grenade launcher, I never saw the gook equivalent of our M-79 grenade launcher, a powerful handy tool built like a sawed-off shotgun, only four times as big around. They break open like a double barrel and lob 40 mm bullet-shaped projectiles up to 400 yards or so that explode on impact. A good M-79 man could carry a hundred rounds. Raven carried between 110 and 120 strung out all across his front and sides. An M-79 man was a walking bomb – one hit in the wrong place could set him off like the Fourth of July, something every M-79 man was very conscious of.

Ground artillery consisted of 105 mm and 106 mm cannons that blow huge holes upon impact. An Ontos is an awesome tank-like creature surmounted by six 106 mm recoilless rifle cannons. When all six were fired at once, the concussion shook the earth for a hundred yards and created momentary vacuum pockets that sucked the life out of lit candles inside nearby tents.

Naval support came from 155 mm and 175 mm howitzers that launch shells bigger around than telephone poles. B-52s dropped 500 pound and 1000 pound bombs that built instant man-made lakes and ponds all over North and South Vietnam. Flame throwers shoot tongues of fire thirty feet or more. LAWs are 66 mm disposable bazookas that can put a Brink's truck to sleep, and anyone stupid enough to stand behind them. Land mines can lift a tractor trailer straight up in the air. Claymores are deadly crescent-shaped, thin bodied anti-personnel mines that blow about 900 small ball bearings covering a 120 degree arc some thirty feet to their front, backblasting for another ten feet or so. Booby traps come in all shapes and sizes and are primarily designed to cause severe wounds to the lower part of the body. It takes four healthy bodies to carry one that's unhealthy.

An unspoken rule dictated that each person carry the maximum amount of weight possible. Helmets weighed four or five pounds. Flak jackets weighed about ten pounds. Grenades weighed about half a pound each. So did bayonets and K-Bars with their sheaths. In or on our packs we carried ammo, C-ration canned food, sleeping gear which included ponchos, rubber mattresses and shelter equipment, an E-tool, a gas mask, a change of clothes if you were lucky, personal effects, extra first aid items and toilet articles. Radiomen carried a .45 caliber pistol and everything any other rifleman carried, except a rifle, plus a twenty-five to thirty pound radio.

Cross-training was an absolute must. Each of us knew the others' jobs. I carried an M-79 for two months (Raven took over from me) and a radio for two months (I took over from Ricky). I also knew how to handle an M-60 machine gun task if necessary, as well as how to fire 60 mm mortars, or LAWs, and how to plant C-4 (a putty-like explosive substance requiring detonator caps). C-4 was very useful for cooking food, or clearing trees so medivac choppers could set down in dense jungle.

-47-

Took a three-day, in-country R & R at China Beach in Da Nang with Raven and Sergeant Rotan in April. Captain Kody frequently sent Raven and Rotan on in-country R & R when he knew we'd be in the rear for any length of time. Said it was to keep them out of trouble. We snuck out to Dog Patch our first night there. Dog Patch was a hole in the ground, a Vietnamese ghetto that was generally off limits to servicemen because of its red-light nature and excessively low-life night club activity. Several GIs who went there never returned. We bribed two sentries to gain passage through the concertina/barbed wire perimeter. Our password was Roger Maris.

Several hours later, while trying to talk our way into a skivvy house, Papa San, standing next to a roll of short bamboo fence stakes, pulled a butterfly knife and denied us entrance, presumably because of our disorderly drunk behavior and because Raven stabbed one of his women in the tit earlier that evening. She and three sleazy-eyed elderly chore-women-by-day, prostitutes-by-night stood in the doorway beckoning Rotan who suddenly struck Papa San with a powerful uppercut that lifted him straight off his feet and back down, ass first and hands-extended-downward flat upon several of the pointed stakes.

The surprised look on his face matched ours. Years of sleeping on a bed of nails wouldn't have prepared him for the excruciating pain that surged through his body microseconds following the neuron-fired thought patterns carrying the seriousness of the situation to his brain. Razor sharp bamboo pierced his ass, thighs, legs, hands and crotch. Blood flowed slowly at first and then quite freely. His screams pierced that night as cleanly as the stake tips pierced his life's essence. Raven, reacting quickly, pulled a grenade and fragged the inside hallway of the skivvy house. High pitched screeching and shrieking jabbed the air all around us, carrying cries of agony clear up over Dog Patch back to camp toward which we fled with all the strength our drunken doped-up bodies could muster.

ROGER MARIS! ROGER MARIS! Raven shouted as we scrambled through the perimeter wire praying the sentries hadn't changed shift. Then, throwing our exhausted selves upon the sandbag wall of the bunker's front gun rest, I caught sight of the reflected moonlight off Raven's teeth, his smile slowly waxing wide in unison with Sergeant Rotan's.

Gimme five, he said, as Rotan and Raven slapped hands.

Did that really happen? I asked myself.

Yeah Buddy, said Rotan, adrenaline rushing through his vibrating body.

That was music to my ears, said one of the sentries, nothing but pure ecstasy.

Like the upper scale on a Stradivarius, said the other.

I spent the next day in my bunk resting and recuperating, the day after that at the beach catching some rays.

-48-

Hey Paisano, called Tony across the squadbay, while moving

rapidly toward my bunk. Did ya hear bout Malcolm? He's in the brig. They rested him for murder or some shit.

I looked at him quizzically, letting it all sink in. Oh no, I thought, surely not. It must have something to do with Troy Richards.

Troy Richards had submitted his Malcolm story to the *Washington Post* and been awarded the Pulitzer Prize for Journalism. Some rival reporter had seen fit to prove the story false, and Richards suddenly found himself disgraced and pounding the pavement in search of work. Rumor had it he swore to get even with Malcolm.

-49-

Baboons, or rock apes, attacked our point squad, one of them climbing and clawing all over David Rickster's back, yanking at his ears and biting at his neck and shoulders. David slammed himself backward against a tree, severely crushing his barking tormentor. Others were throwing sticks and stones at us from behind and high up in trees. Raven blasted four of them with three bloops of his M-79. We backed out of there fast, dusted off Rickster and then moved on, skirting the baboon territory, terrified it would happen again.

-50-

One-two-three-four,
I hate the Marine Corps.
Five-six-seven-eight,
I love pogey bait.
Sound off, one-two.
Sound off, three-four.
Sound off, one-two-three-four.
One-two....threefour.

Got a food and supply package from the Ladies of the Altar Society of Midwest City Oklahoma's Saint Philip Neri's Catholic church on Easter. Emotion flooded my senses. Believing them to be nuns, I sent them something of a well-received written confession. When I got home I discovered to my no slight embarrassment that they had publicized my confession and that they weren't nuns at all, just ladies like my mom doing volunteer work for the church.

One of the gifts was a package of dates, another a box of disposable butane cigarette lighters. Saw three of them blow up within the next month. Took a finger and a half along for the ride.

BIC and Cricket are getting rich experimenting in the Vietnamese market, said Malcolm sarcastically. Matches are damn near useless and Zippos drink scarce fuel. We make damn good guinea pigs is all.

Big fuckin' deal, interjected Marty. What's a finger or thumb in the face of big bucks?

We all looked at him. Marty, gazing back innocently, was just as serious as could be. He wanted to be rich so bad he could taste it, and was among those who believed the ends justified the means.

The problem is, Dumbshit, said Malcolm straight at Marty, as far as the corporate world's concerned we're just like the fuckin' lighters – disposable.

There it is, said C-More. Big companies don't care nothin' about nothin' except profits.

The problem is, Dumbshit, echoed Marty, you dudes all need a fuckin' attitude adjustment. Just wait till we's back on the block and I pull up alongside your cheap-ass Fords in my big bad Rolls. Then we be seein' which tune you dudes dance to.

Hah, laughed Malcolm, you should live so long. The only rolls you be coming up with will be from the bake shop down around the corner. We all laughed, including Marty.

-51-

SHORT ROUND! SHORT ROUND! went the cry some twenty seconds after the preceding FIRE IN THE HOLE shouts.

We dug for cover in frightened frenzy. Short rounds were artillery or mortar shells shortchanged on how much gunpowder had been packed within them. They were dangerous because they landed short. If the artillery field was behind us, there was a good chance the rounds would hit in the midst of our own troops. Some short rounds were so short they never made it out of the perimeter, like the one that shot straight up in the air and straight back down again, landing behind and slightly beneath the compound shitter, blowing the bottom out of the outhouse. Major Dixon came shooting out the side door pelvis first, his pants drooping at half mast hung upon his hardon, his arms and legs pumping for all he was worth, his rod as red as his blushed face, his troops abandoned in laughter, thoroughly jeopardized in the heat of battle. Dixon later conceded he'd been dreaming about Rosy Palm, his sweetheart. But that story's much more personal and best left in Dixon's hands.

Short rounds created terrifying moments of deathly stillness as grown men spoke hurried prayers aloud, the only sounds save those of whistling chunks of metal slicing cleanly through dense airspace parting molecules with themselves. The only consolation was the single thought that the one that gets you is the one you don't hear. I wonder if Jeffrey heard the one that got him. I was a mere three feet to his left cowering in a fox hole and I heard it. I heard it screech Life's a joke – and then you croak. The damage to my hearing still haunts me, a constant reminder of that incident. My ears ring me to sleep at night and wake me in the morning, not always softly, necessarily, like a wake-up call from a whispering loved one, but more often like the roaring whistle of a powerful freight train getting closer and closer until your head feels like it's about to explode.

-52-

Dr. Moronian stood behind the podium in our accounting class one morning preaching that the My Lai massacre was a symptom of the bloodthirstiness so typical of the mentality rampant in our trigger happy armed forces. The Black Molly I'd done an hour or so earlier because I'd been up all night working graveyard shift began to take rapid effect. My twenty-six-year-old brain was racing ninety miles an hour faster than my teeth were grinding.

The class majority was sucking up each Moronian word like it was gospel. I squirmed in place, and then blurted an emotional defense of Lieutenant Calley's men faced with the terror of a search and destroy mission through an enemy-controlled village. And what about the Hue massacre? I added. What about the thousands of innocent villagers butchered by the V.C. and buried in the outskirts of town? No one had heard of that, though, or cared to find out about it.

I believe my spiel lasted a good five minutes, but maybe not considering the effects of speed on one's sense of time and its passage. I'm certain, however, that my lambasting Moronian for his personal opinions negatively reflected in the final class grade I received. Nevertheless, the incident marked a turning point in my life. It was then that I realized most fully how far apart I stood from the majority of classmates I'd compete with in college. I was embarrassed to the hilt. Several bewildered faces turned toward mine. They too seemed embarrassed, ashamed of me even. This was the first time I'd said a word in class, the first time anyone even realized I was a Vietnam Vet, a disease of the first magnitude I supposed then since no one ever sat beside me for the rest of the semester. Thereafter I began growing a black disguise, shoulder length and longer. I nudged my way into society unnoticed when possible and hardly noticed when necessary. Vietnam war supporters were taboo. I wasn't a Vietnam supporter, but I supported supporting the majority of innocent participants so thoroughly exploited by teachings of patriotism and the governments behind it. But I knew I'd only be misunderstood in any attempt to speak about subjects I most of all knew least about. I resolved myself to seek safety through a more passive education, by switching over to the English Department where it was simpler to blend in and easier to escape into other worlds.

One of the very saddest parts to me about my Vietnam experience at that time, was all the lost friendships. I wasn't just thinking of the dead, necessarily, but also those I had never heard from again, or tried to contact for that matter. It's as though each of us had repressed memories that caused great pain and embarrassment. It was easier to forget than forgive I supposed. Now, most of what's left are remembrances of things best forgotten, in one sense. Time, we are socialized to believe, heals all wounds. Vietnam wounds never heal they just hurt less. Time simply encumbers the Vietnam Experience in layers of more and more distanced perspectives. The experience is still as real as the adrenaline it triggers.

-53-

I'm telling you, Lieutenant, when we crossed that ridge we entered Laos. Now you can believe that or not, cuz frankly I don't give a fuck, but right now we're in Laos. Sergeant Travis was angry, and tired of arguing. He had led our platoon for more than three weeks prior to the Lieutenant's arrival. None of us doubted his leadership or ability to read a map.

Lieutenant Little on the other hand had frequently gotten us lost and even more frequently had nearly guided us into the most obvious of possible ambush situations. He was new to our platoon, fresh from Quantico, Virginia, Officer's Candidate School, twenty-two years old, to boot, and convinced that these latter attributes qualified him for the position of leader among men. Determined to prove his woodsmanship, he'd had us wandering aimlessly for days, up hills and down hills, across valleys and crisscrossing valleys, around gullies and into and out of rice paddies and bomb craters, always projecting the appearance, as reflected upon Lieutenant Little's face only, that this particular column of men knew exactly where it was going.

Actually, we did know exactly where we were going but only because Sergeant Travis was something of a built-in compass: plump but not obese, round glasses, pointed nose, shifting eyes, dimples on both cheeks marking east and west, a cleft chin pointing south and a furrowed brow intersected by a vertical scar which, when you skewed your eyes just so, looked like the letter "N" on its side. Lieutenant Little also had the appearance of a compass, the kind used by draftsmen to draw circles: pointed head, spindly legs, scarecrow arms, no chest.

Everyone was on edge. We were burning up, our blood boiling from the terrible heat. It was bad enough wandering around lost in the DMZ, but crossing into Laos was asking for trouble. Rumors had it that US troop buildup was going on someplace called Radar Site 85. Supposedly it was top secret, but everyone knew that wasn't exactly going to keep gooks disinterested. No sir. Eventually they'd overrun it, and then the nearest grunt outfit would be called in for support. We'd just as soon have been as far away from Laos as possible. No choppers would come get our wounded, if need be, nor replenish food and water should supplies run low. Air, artillery or mortar support would be out of the question. The scariest part to me, however, was not being able to distinguish Laotians from gooks. It didn't make much sense to risk becoming the catalyst of another war. Of course, had I known that US presidents can bomb foreign soil without permission from Congress or bomb the countryside of an ally, first without that government's knowledge and then without its permission, I might have felt differently. But I doubt it.

It was early evening when we first saw the river. A narrow bamboo wooden railless footbridge offered the only means of fording it that we'd been able to find since first going up river and then back down, using up most of the daylight remaining. As point man it was my job to cross first and then secure the opposite bank. Agility being one of my strengths, I had no fear for myself, but Benjie I knew was sweatin' it. He didn't swim well, and the water looked deep.

Three or four feet in front of the bridge, in the middle of the slightly overgrown path leading up to and beyond it, I stopped in front of an old pungy-stick boobytrap, slightly washed out by earlier rainfall. I hand-signaled its whereabouts and skirted around but couldn't avoid the small mud patch to its left. Benjie and C-More took up positions to cover my crossing as I cautiously tested my weight on the bridge. It seemed sturdy enough so I began to move, trying hard to stagger my pace as much as possible thinking that might save my life, my logic being that an unpredictable moving target would be that much more difficult to zero in on.

Nearly halfway, I began to feel more sure-footed and picked up a little speed. Quick as a rattlesnake my left foot shot out from under me flipping me straight in the water backwards headfirst. I came up gasping still trying to hold my rifle, which necessity forced me to abandon immediately if I was going to live. The water was definitely deep. I tried to relax but couldn't keep myself above the surface. I looked at Benjie who had risen and darted to the bank. I was tiring fast very fast trying desperately to shed some gear any gear all gear. I went down and fought back up again struggling and thrashing. Thoughts whizzed by like a faulty movie: Benjie on the bridge; C-More's gaze glued to the opposite bank; his rifle pointed and ready; his body yelling in controlled tone for Benjie to stop and be more careful who was getting closer and, more successfully than me, shedding his gear fast. My helmet floated away momentarily, then sank like a turtle, kerplop. I sank too, kicked back up and gurgled Help softly in embarrassment. I couldn't believe it? I was actually embarrassed because I was drowning. I resank with open eyes that stared through clear, still water and fixated on the river bottom boulders overgrown with slimy looking plant-like green life that looked not unlike dark guacamole salad.

People say their life flashes before their eyes at such moments. My death flashed before mine. So did Matt's. I remember thinking Hey, this is it fool. You done did it this time. You're finally going to join Matt. I saw myself sinking and slowly floating downward, getting closer and closer to the bottom which became my grave-yard. I saw myself bounce softly from boulder to boulder, rock to rock, back to boulder to rock, to boulder to rock, again and again, over and over, lightly brushed along, gently skipping with the stream over rocks and stones, roots and logs, when suddenly there was a light, a blinding bright light that penetrated deep into my consciousness, deeper and deeper and around corners and into crevices flooding out my ears and then back in my ears as Benjie's voice calling ROOTIE! ROOTIE! Wake up. Please Rootie. We need you here, helping us, stay alive. And it was Benjie and it was dark and he was gently rocking me and dripping water on my face and speaking softly and there was ground under me, hard ground, and it was real and I was alive, I WAS ALIVE!

-54-

I luf few, she whispered against my ear.

Forty millimeter cannons exploded in my brain as I stroked her thighs, lightly raking her arched pelvis and damp hair. Monsoon rain poured in my thoughts. I fought back to reality. She sweated and shook, then grew clammy and still. Stricklyn was there, in my head, blood and flesh all over the chopper. She gazed up at me through teary eyes not understanding.

I'm sorry, I said. It's not you. I just can't right now.

But you've been back three years now, she sobbed.

-55-

Where'd you ever get a name like Rootie, Rootie?

From Rootie Kazooti, I guess, I said. Shorty started calling me that. Said it was 'cause he couldn't say Rizzuti. I've had nicknames always it seems. In grade school the kids called me Skip, or Skippie, or Skipper. That was 'cause I could skip better than any of the girls even. I loved to skip. It's such a carefree expression, and I always felt so happy then. In high school they called me Rock. That was 'cause I broke out a car window at the Firemen's Field Day in Verona, New York one Saturday night when I was sixteen and me and Keith, my best buddy, we called him Lardo, and Wink, our nose guard, and Heimie, our six-foot-five tightend, were drunk as skunks and feeling malicious. I can't remember if Charlie, our quarterback, was there or not, but anyway four or five huge farm boys came chasing after us. We ran straight across a field and straight into a barbed wire fence and got caught. Monday morning at school Wink started calling me Rock.

Well where'd you get a name like Rizzuti, Rootie? Stricklyn wanted to know next.

It's Italian, man, like you know from Italy. My parents are both Italian. All my grandparents came over from Italy. My mom's folks are both from south of Rome. My grandfather, Tommaso Rossi, was raised in Alatri, an ancient walled city. My grandmother, Angela Capponi, is from San Felice. My dad's folks,

Marco Rizzuto and Rosa Talerino, were from south Italy, from Calabria province, originally from Cape Rizzuto. My family name is actually Rizzuto, but they screwed up my dad's birth certificate and put an "i" on the end of his name instead of an "o." He didn't find out until he went in the Army. By the time he came home from W.W.II, "officially" he was Rizzuti, and I guess he figured it was too much trouble to change it back by then. He talks about changing it back some day. I believe I'll change it myself if he don't. My roots are important to me.

So where'd you ever get a name like Terry, Rootie?

My mom is Teresa and my dad Terigo, even though everyone calls him Phil. Lots of people called them both.... Suddenly a gook came riding a bicycle around a curve and down the trail toward us. Startled, I jumped up yelling HALT. She stopped and I approached, demanding an ID. CUMCHUC! CUMCHUC! I called with heavy emphasis on the second syllable. She reached in her overraincoat-type garment, intensifying the situation momentarily, and stuck out a plastic bag full of papers. Stricklyn stood guarding the gook and the trail. The whole squad had come alive. We had been resting, having humped since early morning. It was just after noon in late November. Her papers are cool, I said. She's fifteen and a student. She lives down in Phu Loc.

Let's blow her away, squirmed Raven, tear her a new asshole.

Yeah, but let's gang-bang her first, came a reply from the rear. She makes my tongue hard, and I'd like her to sit on my dong and teeter totter.

NO! ordered C-More. Let her go.

I motioned for her to leave. Didi... didi mow, I said.

She moved cautiously, walking her bike, eyes darting from the ground to Raven and back to the ground. She was scared shitless and Raven knew it, delighted in it, was ecstatic. Come on! sneered Raven, releasing the M-79's safety and pointing it at her.

Get some, Raven, said the voice in the rear.

Raven was drooling out the corner of his grin, his eyes were absolutely wild, his whole body was wired to the max.

Knock out the shit, Raven, said C-More, pointing his weapon at him. You either be in the Marine Corps or you be a Marine corpse.

What's it gonna be?

Raven just stared at him with that big grin on his face. Un-expectedly, another gook came strolling down the trail from the same direction as the first. He was smiling as he approached, then suddenly flung open his coat and came up firing a small automatic. We dove, except Raven who spun and leaped and fired his M-79 point blank into the gook's gut, blowing him straight up in the air and backwards, spilling his whole insides and part of his back all over the trail; and Malcolm, on Tail End Charlie who, so caught up in the adrenaline rush, likewise leaped instinctively, blowing away the first gook, the girl we'd let go.

Everyone was having a hard time keeping still, vibrating and motor-mouthing way beyond any reasonable and prudent speed limit. There were two dead gooks, and someone I won't name took liberties, and John took an ear and carried it in his wallet until the maggots ate through it and through his trousers and into his ass. He jumped up whooping in the middle of the ambush site we'd set up earlier that night, running in circles and slapping at his ass all at the same time that he was tugging frantically at his cartridge belt so he could drop his drawers. He scared the living fuck out of all of us the same way I did two months later in a similar situation when I realized way too late that I was sitting on top of an ant hill and there were hundreds of them attacking all over my 145 pounds of flesh and bones.

What the hell's eating you? asked Raven.

No gooks walked into our ambushes, that's for sure. At least not often.

> She was comin' around that mountain doin' nothing,
> When the chain on her life cycle broke.
> Well they found her in the grass,
> With a peddle up her ass,
> And her tits all mangled in the spokes.

-56-

Sergeant Hoover ran the squad like an offensive coordinator for a football team, particularly on search and destroy missions through open territory. Center was our M-79 man. Both guards were riflemen. The two tackles carried M-60 machine guns, if we had them (M-16s if we didn't), and both ends carried rifles. Sergeant Hoover and his radioman worked together as quarterback. Behind them depended on what else was available to us, usually the mortar team carrying 60s or 81s if it was a big operation. From this standard formation we could sweep through a village fairly assured of assuming fire superiority. We could work as a wedge, or pivot on either end, or rotate on the middle, or send out flankers to the weak side.

Herb Hoover and I were good friends. He was from Dumas, Texas and proud of it. He boasted lineage with some famous FBI agent and claimed his girlfriend had once been Miss Texas. After seeing the picture she sent him of herself, he sure had me convinced. She was fuckin' gorgeous. Hoover himself was the spittin' replica of the Texas stereotype: Blonde hair, blue eyes, tall and handsome, square jaw and deep Texas drawl. Ahm a ding dong daddy from Dumas, he was fond of repeating. On top of that he was as gung ho as they get. He loved a good firefight. He had two purple hearts and a bronze star for heroism by the time he inherited responsibility as squad leader.

One extremely pitch black night Sergeant Hoover lost the toss in the CO tent drawing straws. Our squad was to go out and set up an ambush. It was so damn dark my eyes never did adjust. Everyone was scared shitless because Charlie controlled the night, and boobytraps are impossible to detect in such darkness. The way I looked at it, though, we could hide in the dark as well as the next guy, and when it's your time to go it's your time. Nothing would change that.

Each of us had a small one-inch piece of reflector tape on the back of our helmets. It gave the guy behind you something to follow. It also gave the gooks something to shoot at I suppose, like the night-luminous wrist watches we wore. I was point man so I couldn't see a thing. About 200 yards outside of camp I walked our whole squad square into an ambush.

Hoover suddenly sensing disaster screeched AMBUSH RIGHT,

and all holy hell broke loose. The noise was suddenly deafening, the flashes blinding. We instantly whirled right and charged on line blasting away, screaming at the tops of our lungs. I dove into a tree trunk nearly killing my own damn self. The confusion stopped almost as suddenly as it had begun. Someone popped a flare: Thoomp... whoosh... pop, and then it gently floated back to earth as it softly whistled its descent. Not a thing moved, not a peep was uttered. We laid there all night waiting till morning before anyone dared budge. As the sun came up and daylight spread, paranoia rose too, cause gooks could play the waiting game better than we could. But this particular plan had been thwarted. Not ten feet in front of us lay four of their dead. We'd sustained no injured, no dead this night.

-57-

Millions of leeches burst forth upon the land in celebration of birth, catapillering their way across the Vietnam spring in huge un-dulating waves, surging their inch-long-hungry-greenish-brown-slimy-bodies over everything in their path, climbing up our boots ascending our bloused trousers thirsting for our blood in droves, motivated by nothing more sophisticated than pure unadulterated survival instinct.

Some leeches have ankle fetishes. Others love soft tummies. All of them will take what they can get: your neck, your lip when you're asleep, your warm moist scrotum, and anywhere within your most creative imagination. Always the telltale sign is the same: inch long thick hickeys all across your bod.

It's very hard to kill a leech. You can't just brush 'em off. You can't pull 'em off either. When they're full they'll drop off. Then you can step on 'em and squish 'em into a pretty good sized bloody mess. Mostly we used insect repellent. That wouldn't kill 'em but it'd make 'em curl up and fall off. We often burned 'em with lit cigarettes. That wouldn't kill 'em either but it made 'em somebody or something else's problem. I'll bet of the hundreds perhaps thousands of leeches I exorcised from my body the same one never visited me twice. One thing I never could figure out though: The natives could snatch a leech off themselves with one swift swipe of either hand. Heredity I guess.

I'll always remember the morning Private Wagner bounded out of the sack, tearing at his buckled up trousers, yanking down his skivvies, screaming LEECHES! LEECHES! MY GOD! THERE'S A FUCKIN LEECH UP MY DICK!

Everybody sorta sat around sleepy eyed for a few seconds, trying to register the seriousness of the situation, while Sergeant Rotan ran to see what the problem was. Wagner was dancing in place, one hand around the back of his dong, the other pinching hold of a leech sticking out the end. He was trying desperately to pull it out, tears running down his face from the pain, the embarrassment and the fear.

CORPSMAN! CORPSMAN! shouted Rotan, frantically pacing around Wagner, reaching out to help, then jerking his hands back, afraid to touch him there.

Frank came running in then and sized up the situation immediately. Hold on, Wagner, we'll get it out. Stay cool. We'll get it out, he said, fixing up a syringe of morphine.

GET IT OUT? yelled Wagner, as Frank shot him up. How the hell we gonna do that, man? You blind or something? Looky here, he said, pulling on the leech, stretching out his dick to what seemed an incredible length.

We'll get it out Wagner, said Frank reassuringly. Just try to relax. I've got experience in these things. We may need to drill or something, but we'll work it out.

Drill? said C-More. No wonder they be calling you dudes corpsmen.

Sounds sexist to me, said Malcolm. They ought to be corpspersons.

Corepussins? said Watson. What the fuck you be talkin' bout?

Never mind, said Malcolm. Too far over your head.

Wagner was laughing hysterically as we put him in the chopper headed for Da Nang hospital. When he got back nearly a month later, he said what scared him most was when he initially looked down: first he thought he was seeing double, then he thought it was Medusa come to turn him to stone.

If I'd known that, said Frank, I'd never have gotten you high.

Been better off if you had turned to stone Wagner, said Malcolm. Even leeches can't get blood outa rocks.

You dudes is pissin' me off royal, said Watson. Always talkin' shit.

Wagner slept with a Band-Aid on his dick from there on out. Every morning we could hear him as he pulled it off, first one end then the other, ooh, ooh. Go ahead, laugh, he'd say, but I ain't taking no chances.

Seems like a rubber'd be easier, said Malcolm.

Never thought of that, said Wagner. CORPSMAN! GOT ANY RUBBERS?

Not *on* me, said Frank.

-58-

Her lips puckered and her eyes drooped. God she was beautiful and I wanted to take her, to force her, but I couldn't move. I couldn't speak. I watched her butt sway toward the door. It opened. Light snow was falling. She put on her coat and stepped out grabbing Jayson and their bags on the way. He was beginning to cry. The door closed softly.

-59-

I remember running into Corporal Lazer at the administration Quonset hut back in Phu Bai my fourth month in Nam. He had gained a lot of weight, and with his short height he actually appeared fat. For a Marine, he looked a disgrace. Cheap paneling decorated the wall behind his desk. A white flower drooped over the edge of a pink vase on his filing cabinet. Soft music came from a speaker I couldn't pinpoint.

It bothered me seeing his Corporal insignia and his starched camouflage utilities. We had gone through boot camp together, and I was still a Private First Class, two pay grades lower. He was pounding a typewriter in an air-conditioned office; I was sweating my ass off beating the bush. To my way of thinking, fairness dictated I should be the corporal and he the PFC; and the grunts should have been wearing camouflage utilities. The only thing he had to hide from was the embarrassment of his choice living conditions.

How'd you make corporal so fast? I asked him.

Easy, he said, dig it: When Headquarters says make a hundred promotions by the end of the month, we make a hundred promotions. Usually what happens is you grunts are all out in the boonies so we have to promote the people back here. It's either that or refuse the promotions, and you know how that is: Nevah Happen, GI.

That figures, I said. You probably do citations the same way. When he smirked and said Of course, I ignored him.

Nine months I spent in Vietnam as a PFC making about $192 a month. I made Lance Corporal in July and my pay shot up to something like $220. A month before I came States-Side I made Corporal, my pay raising to something around $300. Summing it all up, Uncle Sam compensated me about $3000 for thirteen months work. I gave Uncle Sam a pint of blood, two or three ounces of flesh, several quarts of sweat and tears, fifteen pounds of body weight, God knows what portion of my sanity, ten percent of my hearing, according to his measurements, and one tooth. I also gave him the finger every chance I got. Oh yes, lest I forget, let's be fair about this. I did get room and board: C-rations and the open sky. And I did get to keep a couple of pieces of shrapnel in me. And I did come home in better physical condition than I've ever been in in my life.

And presidents get famous making statements like "ask not what your country can do for you, ask what you can do for your country." Well I know exactly what I did for my country, and even more exactly what my country did to me. When the Eagle's constipated the troops just might get the shit kicked out of them, Raven used to say, not to mention the morale. Non Sibi Sed Patriae Sucks.

135

-60-

AH! AH! AH! It was C-More thrashing around gripped in some horribly terrifying nightmare. I shook him. C-More, C-More, wake up man, wake up.

Huh, whuh, he said, jerking up. What's hapnin'?

You're dreaming, C-More, and making all kinds of commotion.

Hue was burnin', he said. The whole fuckin' city was on fire, an inferno. All them beautiful hoes was runnin' round wild, screamin' and hollerin'. That Shell gas station, member it Rootie?

Yeah, I said, what about it?

The "S" was burned off the sign, he said. Only "HELL" was still there, and the whole place was crumblin' down, and dudes was fightin' and gooks was *winnin'*. Gooks was winnin' Rootie!

Take it easy C-More, I said. Calm down man, you be goin' home in ten days. Nothin' ta worry bout then.

Ten days! he said. Ten days! I can't hack it, man. Can't hack it no mo. I'm crackin' up. I gotta get home. I gotta get home see my baby for I die.

I'm really not sure why seeing a Shell gas station seemed so surprising at the time. Oil companies manufacture more shells than arms manufacturers make casings, underwrite more wars than arms produce casualties. Political boundaries are a thing of the past. Only economic boundaries exist. Nixon didn't give a shit about Cambodia.

Tricky Dick: WHAT?

Aggie Agnew: Just what I said, Mr. President, there's North Vietnamese soldiers in Cambodia.

Tricky Dick: Well, what are they doing there? I thought they were supposed to be in South Vietnam.

Aggie Agnew: They cross the border, attack our forces, and then hightail it back to Cambodia where they know it's safe.

Tricky Dick: Well, why is it safe? Why don't we just "blow 'em away" as they say?

Aggie Agnew: Because Cambodia's an ally, Mr. President. We can't just cross their border like that, can we?

Tricky Dick: Sure we can. They did it didn't they? Besides there's no borders up in the air.

Aggie Agnew: (looking perplexed) Do I understand you correct, Mr. President? You want to bomb Cambodia?

Tricky Dick: Let me make myself perfectly clear here, Aggie, send 'em a one way ticket to paradise.

Aggie Agnew: Say what?

Tricky Dick: (looking exasperated) What have I gotta do, spell it out for you?

- blow 'em from here to kingdom come.
- tear 'em to smithereens.
- shoot 'em all to hell and back.
- send 'em on to greener pastures.
- kiss their butts good-bye.
- grease 'em up good.
- rip 'em to shreds.
- give 'em an early out.
- buy 'em the farm.
- make 'em kiss the world good-bye.
- tell 'em it's good-bye Charlie.
- make 'em leave before their time.
- make sure they abandon the show.
- show 'em the door to never never land.
- make sure they bite the bullet.
- have 'em fly the coop.
- force 'em to kick the bucket.
- blow 'em away, goddammit, that's an order!

-61-

Malcolm was pacing the cement cell floor like a black jaguar, his nostrils moist and flaring wide in sync with his eyes. They can't do this to me, Rootie. You know it's a mistake. I didn't murder nobody. Not really. You know that bitch was probably just settin' things up, diverting our attention so that other gook could come down the trail and blow our shit away. And even if technically I did murder her, Rootie, my actions were just a symptom of the

137

larger problem of war. Besides, I paid my dues, man. Can't live like this, not in no cage man, can't be no animal no more. They be talkin' shit, man, talkin' bout sendin' me back to Nam. They can't, man. I'll kill somebody, Rootie. I swear, I'll kill somebody my bare hands.

I looked deep into his familiar eyes and thought back to Hill 602, to within a hundred feet of the compound, to C-More's orders for Malcolm to take out that Korean sentry.

What's a Korean doing here? I whispered.

I don't know, shrugged C-More. Maybe it's a trick, just a gook in Korean uniform.

Or maybe he's North Korean, said Malcolm who shed all his gear, then slowly and quietly snuck up on him, taking what seemed like hours to get there, inching his way forward across the leaves and vines like a frog in slow motion silently stalking a moth, not making a sound, his coveted Gerber Mark II combat knife in his teeth, movie fashion, intermittently flashing in the afternoon sun. The Koreans were head hunters. We all knew that. Koreans took heads like Indians took scalps, symbols of bravery and victory.

The Korean's back was to us, not as it should have been. Had he taken his situation more seriously he'd still be alive – maybe. He was sitting cross-legged on a log several yards away sucking on a cigarette, blowing large circular wisps of smoke that spiraled upward into the stillness and mixed with the mist that seemed to roll in and out and rise up and down at will, sometimes clouding our view of Malcolm, as it did now, when suddenly Malcolm's crossed fists and forearms appeared from the depths, reached up from behind the Korean in slow motion it seemed, and quickly swiped him down off the log in one swift scissors-like movement, then wrestled him into a deadly choke hold position so quickly the only sounds were his rifle slipping down among the branches to his side, the gurgling gasps of spit frothing from between his lips, and C-More and I rushing to assist Malcolm who pulled and pulled, his garrote digging almost as deep in that Korean's neck as C-More's bayonet thrust in his chest, blood spurting out all over high enough to leave one last background impression upon the retinas of his bulging eyes.

Take it easy Malcolm, I told him. I'll talk to 'em, but when I did they told me to stay the hell out of it. Said a murder's a murder. Don't make no difference that when you got time to think about it you don't, and when you don't have time you do. Besides, they had added, Richards is the son of a Doggy, a Full-Bird Colonel up for meritorious promotion. So Malcolm went back to Nam and turned up missing in action.

-62-

Hey man, asked Chris, what's that fuckin' poem you keep recitin'? You know, somethin' about a hundred black stallions?

I'm not sure, I said, it's something I heard a long time ago, back in college. Randy, some redheaded dude in my dorm, used to sing it all the time. In any case I've modified it some and it just keeps going round and round in my brain. I really like it. It's a folk tune.

I like it too, he said. It sounds like something Zimmerman could make famous. I never knew whether to believe him or not, but Chris claimed he and Bob Dylan were roommates in college.

-63-

I got da biggest dick in da whirled!
I got da biggest dick in da whirled!

McKlusky, plastered, was funnier than shit as usual. Six foot seven, about 240 pounds, he looked like a genetic throwback to more primitive times, the kind of guy who'd wipe his ass on a tree trunk if he didn't have no toilet paper, just back right up to it and rub up and down on the bark.

I can't remember laughing so hard as when he came strolling out of the shower in Phu Bai one day, buck naked, his hand wrapped around the base of the biggest flaccid dick I've ever seen, twirling it like Will Rogers working his lariat. People gathered forming a gauntlet on either side of him as he passed through twirling it, shouting I got da biggest dick in da whirled! I got da biggest dick in da whirled!

139

Thirty or forty onlookers went hog raving mad we were laughing so hard. McKlusky's face was huge, like Mt. Washington's, his grin as cavernous as Carlsbad, his teeth meshed stalactites and stalagmites flashing in the bright sunlight, water glistening on his Velcro-kinky black hair.

Obviously, McKlusky had a reputation of sorts. None of the women in any of the skivvy houses would take him on at any price. Rumor had it he once split a woman in two like so much firewood. Screwed up her insides too, I'm told. He never had to worry about Zeke or Jody though, the generic names for the dudes back home doing time with your girl. Nobody could have satisfied McKlusky's girl, other than he himself. Rosey Rottencrotch he used to call her. Said she could suck a golf ball up a garden hose.

-64-

Hey, what's hapnin', home? Ma name's Jerome, man. I be new at this shit. Just pulled in this mornin'. What's gone on down there?

It's a skivvy house, I answered. Captain made a deal with the locals. They get our business; we get laid. Everybody's happy.

What's the goin' rate? he asked.

Five bucks a whack, I told him.

FIVE DOLLARS! How they be making any bread that a way?

Check out the line, I told him. Been like that three days. No slack at all.

The line came straight out the skivvy house door for about sixty or seventy feet, wound all the way around the shitter counter-clockwise and looped back upon itself, forming what looked like from our perspective a very large nine. The skivvy house itself was nothing more than a big box. It had been erected quickly, in less than a day. Inside there were two barely furnished rooms sectioned off by a long narrow hallway, at the entrance to which sat Momma San and Papa San resting on either side like two bumps on a log. Momma San, disinterestedly staring out of large almond-shaped eyes set atop deep dark grooves running the lengths of her cheeks to the corners of her mouth like years of crying had eroded both sides of her face, mechanically controlled the cash flow. Papa San merely observed and handled any dickerin', his black jagged teeth exposed behind an ugly grin, reddish betel juice flowing freely down his thick moist lips and stubble covered chin.

The skivvy house had been built within a sparse grove of short clumpy ming trees. Momma San took great pride in those bushes, every morning and late afternoon watering them down thoroughly till the sand all around them formed a great big oval, drenching water downhill toward the shitter.

What kinda trees those be? asked Jerome. Why she be waterin' 'em so regular?

They're ming trees, I told him, an aphrodisiac. They need lots of humidity to survive.

Ming trees, said Jerome pensively. What's aphrodisiac?

I don't know, I said, somethin's supposed to make you horny.

Ha! he laughed, outa fuckin' sight! No wonder all the splib dudes be up front. I knowed aphrodisiac must be somethin' bout blacks.

By mid-afternoon the evaporation off the ming trees would form a misty cloud all around and above the skivvy house, shielding the entrance from view. The leaves would swell up and be soft to the touch. Gentle pressure would result in moisture dripping down long slender fingers. By late afternoon the cloud would have lifted and the leaves would start to contract. It was at about this time that Momma San would begin the whole watering process over again, and the two working ladies inside changed shift with two fresher ones from the village. No one could see what went on at night, but everyone assumed it was more of the same, since all the diehards, the gluttons for punishment, could still be seen standing in the line that seemed to have no end, going in one end and coming back out the same entrance, infinitely looping back upon itself like Kekule's dream.

-65-

Les, I whispered.

Say what, he said.

Is that hummingbird sittin' still? I asked, or is it the dope?

141

It's sittin' still, he said.

Wow! I thought, I've never seen a humming....HEY LOOK! there's another one, OH WOW LOOK there's a third! Jesus, hummingbirds were all around and above us, hovering and flitting here and there, taking turns resting in the small bush-like flowering trees surrounding our listening post, beautiful aqua marine back-sides, zigzagging in and out of each other's flight paths as though they were sonar-equipped chimney bats, tongues flicking in and out of needle-nose beaks, lapping up nectar like puppies weaning on milk.

At one point I counted twelve, but then it looked as though there were fifteen or twenty, and then there were only six or seven, and then fifteen or twenty again, and so on until Raven walked up, and then there were none.

I ain't never seen no flowers over here, said Raven, pointing out the trees. He was right; I hadn't either come to think of it.

Only ones I ever seen, said Les, were all dead. It was the strangest thing. It was that time we were way the fuck out by Quang Tri and taking all that shit from them snipers. There was a whole field of dead flowers, like tulips, and they was on little mounds in rows, and they was standin' up bent over wavin' in the wind. Reminded me of a bunch a old grave stones.

There doesn't seem to be all that many animals over here either, I said, considering it's a perfect habitat for nearly everything.

Nearly everything except us, said Les. Guess all the noise scared 'em into Laos or Cambodia or something.

Raven took a hit and then another in quick succession. Cover me, Rave, I said as I seated myself on a rock and started breaking my weapon down to clean it.

Sure, he said, checking the chamber on his M-79 and quickly scouring the perimeter.

My rifle's fuckin' filthy, I said. It was also wet and beginning to pick up a light surface rust. The magazines didn't look much better, so I pulled out all the rounds and began scrubbing them too. I looked at Raven's profile, studying his jet black hair, from which he got his nickname, although he liked to say it was because he was a ravin' lunatic. He was picking his nose and wiping snot on his trousers. We'd all gotten a little lax in our social graces, but it never seemed to bother him the least whether anyone noticed. Curious, I thought, I don't even know his real name. All I know is he's from Fredericksberg, Virginia.

Where's the ambush site tonight, Rootie? he asked, interrupting my thoughts and handing me a plastic bottle of gun oil.

I don't know, I said, but C-More didn't seem too pleased with the overlay, so we'll probably go somewhere else.

C-More was one of those squad leaders who seemed to have a sixth sense for where not to set up an ambush. He learned that from Seldom who learned it from Sparky the dog who rode atop his pack wherever we went. He called him Sparky the day they met, white phosphorus burning a hole in his leg so bad sparks were shooting out. Seldom cut his leg off, just snapped it in two with a pair of wire cutters. Sparky paid him back by whining every time we set up an ambush somewhere he didn't like. We'd move until Sparky felt comfortable enough to sleep. It made sense that when an ambush site seemed risky to Sparky, Seldom led us somewhere else close by. It had to be close so we wouldn't worry about running into our own guys and being mistaken for gooks. If we did get caught in the wrong place, it was easy to say we got lost in the dark.

The scheme worked fine until one night when twenty-eight gooks filed past our "wrong" ambush site. They were extremely heavily armed North Vietnamese Regulars: machine guns, mortars, the works. There were only seven of us, sittin' there shittin' our pants wonderin' whether to open up on 'em or not. We all waited for C-More to fire first, figurin' that would be the signal. What we didn't know was C-More was sound asleep, sittin' up catchin' some Z's.

All twenty-eight gooks were square in our ambush, easy picking so to speak. Les got so nervous he squeezed the clackers on the claymores by accident, setting in motion a series of events that lasted well over an hour. C-More came alive firing before his eyes were even open. Tracers flashed like miniature fireballs. Flashed so brightly they could have lit up Fifth Avenue in the Big Apple. By the time it was all over it was a damn good thing because we were all out of ammo, and the Lieutenant back at the CP didn't have any idea whether to provide support because he had no inkling what was going down out there in a place where there wasn't supposed to be anybody.

The next morning there were sixteen dead gooks and one wounded. Raven made it seventeen dead gooks. Did him a favor, really, fucked up as he was. Two were White Russians. Four were women. One carried the payroll. Another carried a child, papoose style. That was pretty sad, but we all pretended not to see. Lance Corporal Beardly got his third purple heart that night. Not because he was wounded but because he had purposefully jabbed his left arm several times with a C-ration can opener. Nobody said anything 'cause we were all too happy to see him get to go home. Two hearts is enough for anyone; three is overkill.

-66-

One of my most frequently asked questions was: What do you do in the Marine Corps when you're not in a war zone? My standard answer was: You practice war games so that when you are in a war zone you'll have some idea how to react, or so the theory goes anyway. Now, let's examine this a minute. Here you've got thousands of men who've just returned from Vietnam, and what are they doing here in the states? Why they're playing war games in preparation for going back to Vietnam. (The threat of a second tour was very real.) And they're practicing those war games under the command of others who lack previous war experience.

Now, try to imagine how many Vietnam Vets went AWOL, or were busted, or thrown in the brig, or dishonorably discharged for such offenses as sleeping on hole watch, refusing what seemed like silly orders, throwing fists with one another, or any number of related charges. Subtract from those men all the rest of us and you've got two remaining categories: Boots (gung ho ignoramuses who couldn't wait to go to Nam) and Salts (short timers and long timers so wrapped up in apathy they'd do anything to get out). By the time Early Outs were granted for Vietnam Vets, sometime in late 1968 or early 1969, thousands of lives had already been

144

ruined.

Thousands also were promoted in Nam, creating an extremely top heavy states-side organization when those same men came home. Many of us returned as corporals and sergeants. That meant that time-in-grade became the determining factor in the chain of command, the implication being that there were far too many lords and hardly any peons.

Many of us also came home to face another two and a half years of remaining military service on our original four-year enlistments. This situation created severe morale problems. Sergeants and corporals were ordering sergeants and corporals around. Corporals were committed to shit details that ordinarily would have fallen to privates and PFCs. Boot lieutenants and high ranking NCOs with no Nam experience were placed in charge of whole companies of Vietnam War vets.

Corporal Potter came home after a full tour to find his wife five months pregnant waiting to break the news to him. Henslow's girl had married someone else but sent him daily love letters all the while he was gone. Smitty's single-parent mom had packed up and moved while he was gone, leaving no forwarding address. The neighbors said she just up and disappeared one night with all her belongings.

Potter punched his wife in the stomach just before he knocked out two of her front teeth. We sent two brig runners to New York to fetch him out of jail. Henslow cried every night, drinking his way into oblivion, committing suicide eventually, along with some ungodly number of other Vieterans.

Ronnie's and Waynes's wives asked them for divorces when they got home. Sergeant Newcomb's pet Toy Collie ran away from home the same day Newcomb left for Nam. His parents didn't have the heart to tell him until he got home. James Saligar's father sold James' pride and joy while he was gone, his '57 two-door hardtop Chevy.

Roscoe followed his balls down the aisle and married a gorgeous eighteen-year-old he'd only known two months. Just stood there at the altar like an amateur bowler at the foul line glued to what looks to be a perfect strike. He stood stiff and erect, his sixteen-pounder hooking rapidly across the slick surface of his mind, slipping into the crease. He fired into the air, he imagined, as all ten pins exploded on impact. Bout fucking time, he thought as the priest, arriving late, positioned himself to utter the famous words: We are gathered here before all mighty God....

-67-

She hadn't looked back. I moved my eyes toward the window as their shadow passed by and then parted my lips. I opened my mouth to yell, to call her back, to tell her what Nam was like, but no sound came out, only a tremble and then a tear and then several tears and then convulsions followed by silence and that haunting single thought I'm alone again, I'll always be alone. I know now it could never have worked out. I think I knew then I'd never see them again.

-68-

And Captain Kody said You *will* give to United Way.
 And I refused.
 And Captain Kody said You *will* give to United Way.
 And I refused.
 And Captain Kody, taking a deep breath, asked Why? It's only a dollar.
 And I answered Because of those Care packages we found addressed to Hanoi, sir.
 And Captain Kody said I *will* have 100 percent participation, Lance Corporal.
 And I said I refuse to give my money to them, sir.
 And Captain Kody said You've got six seconds to sign this card son, and that's an order.

And I signed that card, donating one dollar, but not before thinking back to the mess I got myself into over a lousy fifteen cents. I wasn't about to find out how much trouble a whole dollar could buy, especially from Captain Kody, a huge shaven-headed

146

full-blood Cherokee who looked like he just came down off the Trail of Tears. Captain Kody was a born leader, a cross between Yul Brynner and Telly Savalas. I remember the Hill Fights on Operation Kingfisher when we got our asses waxed up near Con Thien in the DMZ. I should clarify that somewhat; we did some butt stompin' our own damn selves. That was when practically nobody brought their flak jackets and helmets. It was hot all right, but not as hot as later when the shit hit the fan.

We had moved our company of 129 men into a large circle like a wagon wheel and begun digging in for the night around a small rocky knoll. The mortar teams were spread out like spokes. The command post formed the hub. Captain Kody had just pulled off his backpack and was unbuckling his cartridge belt when two gooks suddenly popped up out of a spider trap right in the middle of the perimeter.

Quicker than Billy the Kid, Captain Kody drew his .45 and blew 'em both away before anyone else even knew what had happened. Then, as though by signal, the mortars and rockets started coming in from several directions, and all hell broke loose. At first, everyone just stood around like Eskimos watching the third world war. Then everybody started scrambling fast, trying to dig deeper, but the ground was half rock. Jeffrey and I dove in side-by-side mortar holes praying lightning wouldn't strike twice in the same place when the first choppers came in after wounded. The mortar barrage increased intensely. Captain Kody called in artillery and air support, and five minutes later the INCOMING shouts went up followed by SHORT ROUND shouts as the first shells came down in the vicinity of the enemy stronghold, all but one that is, the one that took Jeffrey on an early-out clause, leaving us nothing but a hole to remember him by.

Missing in action, or dead? asked Raven.

You call that one, I told him. I call it sad.

Dark set in but incoming mortars kept up all night. We dug and dug until our E-tools got dull and the blisters got so bad we could hardly use our hands. Light rain began to fall, and then dumped, and then quit, and then the mosquitoes came out in droves. I doused myself head to toe with repellent, but they attacked right through it. Illumination rounds and flares were bursting all above us, turning our whole world into a shadowy surrealistic setting of figures and objects flitting here and floating there. The wind picked up, evaporated our soaked clothes, and made it unbearably cold.

Sometime around four in the morning it got extremely quiet. Whispers passed all the way around the perimeter and came back like echoes. HEADS UP.... HEADS up.... heads up.... heads.... For an hour and a half we sat there straining to see when suddenly the first wave moved in, initially as shadows only, and then as crouched dark gorilla-like figures silhouetted against the dawning sky, spraddling the horizon. They came at us in a short burst by what seemed like hundreds, thick like briar bushes. We mowed 'em down and they kept on coming so we brush-hogged some more. But they kept on coming like roaches in the night.

It was nearly daylight when they disappeared the first time, dragging their dead and wounded off with long-handled meathooks arching high in the air, snapping down like cracking bull whips, deep into rib cages for better, longer-lasting holds. That was when I became conscious of our first serious problem. We had a lot of dead and wounded, and gaps in our perimeter. The medivac choppers arrived about the same time the mortars began again. We threw the wounded on board as quickly as possible and then tightened our perimeter defense. The problem with tightening the perimeter was that we had to abandon the holes we'd dug. Fortunately, there were several deep mortar holes to choose among.

Minutes later that seemed like hours the mortars quit, so Captain Kody passed the word to stay alert but chow down. I quickly broke out a can of beans and franks and gobbled them cold. Next I opened a can of peanut butter and wolfed that down.

You fuckin' A right, laughed Raven, a can a day keeps the shits away.

I grinned, then opened a can of fruit cocktail and sucked down the hot juice. Raven set up his makeshift stove, heated some coffee and shared it with me. I passed him the uneaten fruit cocktail, and he hurriedly scooped it into his mouth using two fingers.

You're a goddamn animal, I said, laughing.

So who gives a flying fuck? he said.

Me, Raven, I kidded. Don't want nobody comin' around my house back in the world unless my folks can be proud of 'em.

Hey, he said, I'm a fuckin' war hero, man. Everybody loves a war hero. They even make 'em presidents and shit.

Shit maybe, I said. But there ain't no presidents comin' outa this war, Raven.

GET DOWN NEBRASKA! I screamed as the next wave moved toward us blowing bugles and stampeding like cattle, gruntin' and groanin' so loud that that in itself was scary. Nebraska was going crazy running from hole to hole lobbing grenades and firing his rifle, zigzagging all around the perimeter like he was riding fence line. I was slamming magazines in my rifle and burping rounds out parallel to the ground like they were going out of style when suddenly the gooks just disappeared again and it grew quiet, deathly quiet. My heart was thumping so loud my ears hurt, pounding so hard my flak jacket burst forward with each beat.

I pulled out a cigarette and watched my shaking hands light it. It seemed as though they belonged to someone else. I dragged on it, slowly and deeply, watching the ash rush halfway up its length and feeling the smoke swell my lungs and then release out my nose. Raven stared at me out of scared lifeless eyes and I wondered if I looked the same to him. He nodded, his mouth scrunched up, as though reading my thoughts.

Let's watch each other's backside, Rootie, he said. If it's gotta be now, I want us to be the last ones down.

Okay, I agreed, but what's so important about being last?

Then I can go out feeling like a winner, he said, like I done my best better'n any a these other fuckers.

AMMO CHECK! screamed Captain Kody to the two remaining squad leaders. That was when I became aware of another very serious problem – we were running low on ammo, and the supply choppers wouldn't come anywhere near us. I only had two magazines left, so I switched over to semi-automatic, then sat down and buried my head in prayers.

Give me strength in my roots, I said, give me strength in my

roots:
I am Terry, Son of Terigo, Son of Marco and Rosa;
I am Terry, Son of Teresa, Daughter of Tommaso and Angela.

Nebraska was bubbling with energy, going around collecting grenades off dead bodies, rigging booby traps in the holes we'd dug. Raven, all out of M-79 rounds, was trying desperately to refamiliarize himself with a rifle, practicing changing magazines, when the third wave came at us in pairs of two.

Captain Kody came down and joined us, side by side, carrying a rifle. Nebraska jumped up and out in spite of my attempt to hold him back, pitching grenades at machine gun sites as fast as he could pull the pins, yelling and screaming STRIKE ONE GOD-DAMMIT! STRIKE TWO... when suddenly a .31 caliber blew his brains out. I saw them paint the sky, momentarily, a dull overcast gray. He pitched forward trying to lob one last hook shot that landed at his own feet, blowing his legs out from under him.

I crawled and scrambled to him quickly. NEBRASKA! I shouted, as snot shot out my nose all down my chin.

Momma, Momma, he moaned softly. Call my Momma, Rootie, he whimpered. Blood dripped out his nose and ears. Liquid grayish-white sauce poured out the side of his head all down my shirt sleeve.

SUDDENLY THERE ONE WAS: A GOOK! I'd never seen one so close before. He looked surprised too, and younger than me. His slant eyes turned wild and round. I was all outa balance, but I swung my rifle around hard by the sling. It caught him upside his head, knocking his helmet off thudding to the dirt. He tried to recover to bring his weapon around but I moved fast, like coming outa the blocks in track, swinging my rifle harder and faster, knocking him down. I kept on swinging, beating him harder and harder in a flurry – leftrightleftrightleftrightleft.

Suddenly there was Raven with his E-Tool arching high in the sky, descending through the clouds like an eagle slashing effort-lessly through the gook's neck, flinging a divot of flesh lobbing through the air like a nine-iron shot to the green. I couldn't stop beating him till Captain Kody yelled, HE'S DEAD! HE'S DEAD!

and the shouts echoed like screams in a cave.

Back to the hole I dodged and dove as Captain Kody jumped up, his face strained dark red, and fired at a gook headed straight at our hole. Captain Kody's first shot caught the gook's shoulder and twisted it back, but he kept on coming. He fired again, point blank at his chest, ripping it open but he kept on coming, dropping his rifle as he ploughed forward still on hands and knees. Kody drew his .45 and plugged him in the leg that shot out from under him spinning him up and around and down a full three-sixty flat on his face, but still he crawled at us, clawing the ground before him, his face contorted beyond humanness, his voice growling low. He died clutching the front of our hole, his eyes stretched open, his tongue twitching between black teeth, opiated betel juice drooling down and out from between thick, blood-stained, trench-mouth looking lips.

Air strikes and artillery scattered the remaining attackers. Napalm turned the perimeter into a smoking wasteland filled with stench. Choppers came in with supplies of ammo, water and food, dusting off dead and wounded in exchange. We walked out three days later, 97 totally exhausted men, forty-nine of them walking wounded, filing out past 150 or so scared shitless replacement troops.

Here, you'll need this, I said, offering my flak jacket to someone, a clean-shaven Cherry whose hands were trembling and boots were still black.

No thanks, he answered. It's too damn hot.

I've always wondered if he made it home. Operation Kingfisher left three hundred and forty Marines dead, three thousand eighty-six wounded.

Terry P. Rizzuti

PART 3

IN THE END

Terry P. Rizzuti

PARANOIA PLUS

What are you going to do when you get back, Rootie? asked Father Kelsey.

Guess I'll go on finish my time, then go to school, I told him. I'm gonna write a book about this someday. I'm gonna tell the whole world how this ain't right. Ain't right be pumpin all us boys up then blow us away like this.

Good luck to you, he said. May God go with you.

Wish they all could, I said, raising my voice as he walked away and I turned to board the plane.

Mixed emotions I endured the day I left Phu Bai, November 7, 1967. My outfit was in the boonies so there was no send off, except for the Chaplain stopping to say good-bye. I wanted to be excited but that's difficult when there's no one around to share in the good fortune. Even when someone shouted SEVEN DAYS, to let everyone within hearing know how short he was, I didn't yell out with the customary response to let him know that compared to me he still had a lifetime to go.

I spent a restless night in Da Nang, bedded down with others in my situation, thinking about Raven and Malcolm who only had twenty days to go, and dwelling on the fact that I was abandoning them here. I felt guilty about that, and for the first time I understood why some guys stayed for a second tour. The others also knew no one, and were experiencing similar pangs of guilt. It all caused very strong feelings of anxiety, much like birth and death: Just the same as one enters this world alone and then leaves alone, so too we arrived in Nam alone, came home alone and that year in between seemed like a lifetime. We boarded the plane for Okinawa, some fifty or sixty strangers squeezed like sardines into a C-130 cargo space. I remember staring out the ass-end loading ramp through the fog in my brain...

The stench was unbearable. Only the coke addicts weren't wearing handkerchiefs like bandits. Someone up front yelled Jesus, look at this. Pieces of raw reddish maggot-infested flesh were everywhere scattered on the ground and in the trees. Flies buzzed by the thousands, banging up against our skin and sticking to our clothes. The C-130's tail section, separated from the rest of the plane, was embedded in thick jungle foliage some fifteen or twenty feet in the air. Charcoaled bodies still smoldered, limbs frozen in vivid gestures, sizzling hair receding rapidly before the advance of smeltering flesh.

Everyone suddenly went nuts grabbing money and jewelry, looting the plane and the bodies. Several people were puking their guts out, retching and heaving globs of undigested food. Our job was to bag up the remains so they could be heli-lifted out. I grabbed some dude's arm to drag him out of the wreckage, but it came loose from the socket and pulled away in my hand like a drumstick from a well done turkey. I tried to thrust it back, but it felt stiff, springy and strange. The skin on his face had already grown tight, like a condom drawn over a shell casing, and his teeth were bared in that hideous grin at death.

Nearby lay another corpse with a cigarette butt in its mouth burned down to the filter. It was intensely nauseous, and the whole situation turned dream-like and vague. I wallowed in that gory harvest as though looking through the bottom of a whiskey bottle. Everything blurred and became surrealistic, imposed randomly on a lush green background. Disassociation came like an airborne disease from the others around me experiencing similar distancing reactions. We became automatons, rapidly tossing and shoveling dismembered bloated bodies and parts of bodies into piles for easy, fast collection.

Our return to Phu Bai was met with shock. People ran from our approach unable to deal with the stink. Even our Chaplain uncharacteristically failed to greet us upon our return. I stood in a cold shower for nearly an hour, scrubbing and rescrubbing, but the smell stays with me always, and the images are burned deep. The hairs in my nostrils vibrate or quiver when I think about it; my nose stings like just before a sneeze; I shake at the thoughts, then, and my bones seem to rattle. They burned our clothes in a huge bonfire, then sent us out on a fresh mission.

November 10, 1967, on the Marine Corps birthday, time traveled backwards as we headed east out of Okinawa toward the California coast. It always goes by fast when you're having fun, snickered the Seabee seated beside me. Some guys seemed pretty exuberant on that flight. Most of us, however, remained rather subdued. All sorts of things raced through my brain.

What's it like to pass through Customs?
Where will I be stationed next?
How long will it take to get us there, to the land of the big PX?
How much leave time will I have?
What are my folks thinking right now?
Wish I could parachute into their backyard.
How will I get home without money?
Will student activists greet our arrival?
What's changed back home?
Will there be a homecoming, a brass band?
Am I really going home?
Is this a dream?
Was Vietnam real?

-2-

My last 100 days in Nam are the most unclear to me. The closer I got to my departure date, my drop dead date, the more paranoid I became, shutting down sensitivity to all but the most persistent of input. C-More was down to ten days by that time and couldn't sleep at all at night. By NINETY DAYS I was a bundle of nerves.

C-More got on the plane in trepidation. The nervous grin spread to one side of his face exposing the gold tooth I so well remember. He turned as he ducked inside the plane and waved quickly. I thought I saw moisture in his eyes but probably not. C-More fought that sort of thing as effectively as he did gooks. I'm sure it was just a reflection off the tears in my own eyes.

-3-

Dear Me, 10 Aug 67

I've already written you once today, but for some reason I feel the need to talk to someone and you're the only one I can turn to. I don't know exactly what's bothering me, but I'm scared stiff. C-More's gone home and I'm so scared and jumpy my hands shake whenever I hold them up and look at them. I've only got 90 days to go. It's like 90 years. I swear it is.

We're supposed to move north again in September. Word has it Khe Sanh, the Rock Pile, Camp Carol, Camp Evans, Dong Ha, Con Thien or the DMZ. There's thousands of them up there, thousands. And there's no telling how long we'll be there. Do you know the odds against me surviving up there. They're a hundred to one I'll be killed or wounded again. I can't stand it no longer. I'm cracking apart. My mind's gone ape-shit. I jump whenever someone just snaps his fingers. I've been there before and it's hell.

It's pure hell. You watch your buddies fall like flies, and all the time you hear some gungy officer screaming "Push on, we're Marines." And each time I want to say "Fuck the Marines. I wanna go home. I ain't no hero." But it's no good. I joined an outfit with a reputation constantly being preserved. The 26th Marines took Iwo Jima. God, if I go up there again I'll go berserk. My mind will crack. It's got to. A person can only take so much and then something must give.

I've come so far. To have it all end my last two months seems so meaningless – so much in vain. I can't die now; it doesn't make sense; I've got too many things to do. And yet death looks so close. It's staring us all in the face like so many clouds. I can't stand it. Everybody else is so new. Half of them have never even been shot at. They're all boots, *boots*! Do you know what that means? It means they're all gonna be looking for me to tell them what to do, to show them. I can't show them, not anymore. I can't show them without becoming some sort of John Wayne. And yet if I don't they'll think I'm a coward. I'm not a coward, but it's time to play safe. It's time to come home, but they're all so innocent. They haven't even lost their baby fat yet. I can't let them down. I just can't.

But then, I can't let you down either, or my friends, or my family. Oh God what should I do? You've got to help me. I'm going out of my gourd. There's thousands of gooks up there. And they've got every weapon we've got. And they're all North Vietnamese-trained soldiers. And they all smoke that opium which gives them some ungodly amount of courage.

I need help, and you're the only one I can turn to. I love you so much and yet, believe it or not, if I were to lose an arm or leg I'd see to it that I never saw you again. That's a hard thing to say but it's true. I couldn't face you again. Please help me.

Love, Rock

-4-

It was important to us in Nam to always be men, to be brave no matter the cost. One of the most difficult things we faced was tight-rope walking that delicate ground between caution and cowardice. NOBODY wanted to be a coward, yet nearly everyone wanted to stay alive without having to be too brave either. It wasn't enough to just keep going; courage couldn't be found in the mere act of putting one foot in front of the other. Difficult as that was, we never really felt like we had any choice. And some things were just so intrinsically expected of you, like going out under fire after the dead or wounded; doing them didn't make you a hero even though not doing them made you a coward.

Another problem was that fine line that separates fear from rage. Sometimes fear rose to such uncontrollable, such unbelievable levels, suppression and sublimation only succeeded in converting it to anger – anger at your own blindness for placing yourself in such a predicament in the first place; anger at your country's Madison Avenue sales approach to the military lifestyle; anger at the gung-ho lifers who don't give a shit about anything except their own career advancements; and anger at the Viet Cong for providing what seems at the time like the only legitimate means of dissipating that rage. By the time I was down to EIGHTY DAYS I lived seconds away from a breakdown I felt certain was coming.

-5-

Since our days were numbered, we kept personal calendars. Short timers calendars we called them. Mine was an outline of a naked woman. I carried it everywhere. Her anatomy was segmented into puzzle-like pieces numbered from zero to 395, each digit representing one day of the thirteen-month tour. At first I shaded in whole sections beginning with 395 and working downward. Her breasts were numbered two and one, her you-know-what was zero. By the time I hit SEVENTY DAYS not a morning went by without my carefully unfolding that calendar to repeat the ritual of deleting one more day.

-6-

In one way in particular, GI's had it better during World War II. They had the hope of the nation, most of the world even. They had hope that the war could end any day due to victory. Of course in another way in particular, World War II GI's had it worse. They had to worry about enemy bombs. We only had to worry about our own bombs.

I heard the big B-52 droning back to base one night when our squad had set up an ambush. It was returning from a bombing run up north and released its unspent 500 pound payload less than half a klick west of us. I listened to the whistle screaming of its descent until blinded by the flash. I found myself raised from a sitting position straight up in the air a good two feet some second or two before I felt the concussion and the quake and heard the subsequent roar. My nose started pouring hot blood down my chin.

FUCK ME! yelled Roger at the same time Raven said Well kiss my ass.

They just did, someone answered.

I am thoroughly convinced I could not have dealt well with bombs. Artillery, rockets and mortars were already eroding my ability to cope. I understood why bombers couldn't return to base carrying payload, but Jesus Christ why couldn't they have dropped their leftovers in North Vietnam, or in the ocean?

-7-

By SIXTY DAYS rumors were spreading that Khe Sanh was coming. Hill 881 would be the objective. Nobody knew what Khe Sanh really meant, or 881, but we felt certain it was BAD, because the officers were all nuttin' up, balls in their throats, all on the rag at the same time. I had looked at Raven who looked at me shrugging as if to say It can't be any worse than Hill 602.

We had been six yards outside the concertina wire on 602, all of us on line waiting for C-More to signal CHARGE when a US Army Major stepped out from around a hut. Behind him walked a Captain carrying a radio. I had never seen a Captain carry a radio before. We pulled back to regroup and think through what was happening. C-More ordered me and Shorty to play recon, so we waited for dark and then snuck across the wire into the compound, working our way toward the window of an antenna-covered building.

Inside our discovery had been five US Army officers seated around a poker table playing bid whist. One was a Lieutenant Colonel. Against a far wall were three radios set up to receive distant signals. Kill ratios and other statistics were written all over free-standing chalk boards. Some gorgeous half-clad chick was changing albums on a record player. The Lieutenant Colonel was talking, looking bored and plaintive. There was a murmur of concurrence when the Major we'd seen earlier entered the door. We could hear the Colonel ordering the Major to move his ROK (Republic of Korea) scouts further down slope. Yes sir, said the Major, snapping to attention and saluting smartly. Shorty and I had beat feet out of there fast, like there was no tomorrow, grabbing the others on a dead run.

Coming down off 602 the next day, crashing through jungle so thick it seemed like dusk instead of mid afternoon, we penetrated dreamland. Gnarled vines as big around as fire plugs spun upward, disappearing into the triple-canopied tree tops standing guard above, spreading nets of camouflage, shielding the floral underworld. Cascading water rushed downward, banking furiously around bends, bobsledding toward the rice paddies flooded on the valley floor. Huge stepping-stone boulders offered our only means of further downward penetration. Gorgeous ferns spread windmill-size leaves outward like protruding ribcages. Tall onion-like grasses waved about the river banks, onlookers at our parade. Very large fish leapt and dove, leapt and dove. I stood in awe, the natural beauty jangling against the backdrop of imminent war.

Wiskey swung down and out onto the first rock, his Tarzan cry barely perceptible above the roar of the river, each of us in turn following suit, swiftly leaping boulder to boulder till, unexpectedly, Stricklyn lost his balance and smacked his buttbone hard, judging by the agony in his face, his rifle slipping and sliding banging and bouncing metal and wood against rock and stone, disappearing finally into the depths below. He sat there leaning on one leg praying and cursing the pain away. We held our laughter till he could move again, then busted guts the whole rifle-retrieving mission.

Beautiful birds swooped in strange loops inches above the foamy water and the bright mossy-green rocks, snatching insect life in medias res, their sunset colors flashing and glittering first here then there like fire flies in dim moonlight. I stood meditating, sensing the mystery, convinced of the possibility of transporting myself home if I could just believe enough, if I could just tap into the power somehow and find the key to that door Benjie and I spoke of so often.

I remember stopping for a smoke break, snorting some old roaches that is, and staring at the boulder beneath me, at the spot where an Oriental beetle appeared suddenly, scurrying in figure eights, hot on the trail of a large black ant trying desperately to get away, to get home. He made the entrance of a hideout just a split second ahead of the beetle but not before losing a hind leg. I remember watching him crunch down on that leg, imagining I could hear the sounds of crackling bones, when about a two or three inch chunk of stone disappeared beside him, and then another and a third before I realized it was rifle fire and I was targeted for destruction. Everyone else realized it about the same time too, all nine of us again hightailing it downward, although more sure footed now than ever before.

We were nearing bottom when the river finally quieted. Stopping to listen for our pursuers, we heard nothing. Boottop high, thick, leech-filled grass separated us from the blacktop road leading out. Hill 602 loomed at our backs, menacingly shadowed at the top. I turned to give it a salute in my mind, satisfied to have survived the three-day climb and descent. The lieutenant was pissed when he learned where we'd gone, but C-More was his favorite squad leader, and since we'd taken no casualties he got over it quickly enough.

I'd give anything for a beer, said Shorty.

Yeah, agreed Raven, except a one way ticket home or a pink ID card, or a round-eyed piece of ass for that matter, he added as an afterthought.

-8-

YOU DID WHAT? screeched both my parents at once when I told them I'd joined the Marine Corps and would be leaving for San Diego at six the next morning. That night me and my buddy Dick picked up two friends, both named Mike, and went bar-hopping around Norman. Plastered out of our minds, I mean like totally ploughed, we discovered at about two a.m. we were all out of beer.

One of the Mikes knew of a place out on east Alameda where

you could get served after hours, so we drove there. The place was dark and deserted. There was an outside doorbell-buzzer with a sign over it saying "Ring for Service," so I pushed it. A few minutes later a sleepy-eyed forty or fifty year old man slid open a big door-sized window revealing himself and part of the interior. I asked him for a six-pack and he asked for $2. Most six-packs were only about a buck and a quarter so I questioned the high price. He said Take it or leave it so I dug around in my pocket coming up with less than a dollar. I asked him to wait a second while I went back to the car for more money. Among the four of us we only managed to rustle up $1.85.

I walked back to the window where the beer sat on the ledge but the proprietor was gone. In one of those split-second stupid decisions I left the $1.85, grabbed the six-pack and ran to the car. Jumping inside I started her up, peeled backwards spraying gravel all over the undercarriage, then yanked the wheel right hard and threw it in first gear just as Mike yelled QUICK! DUCK! HE'S GOT A FUCKIN' GUN!

All four of us ducked, including me, as I jabbed my foot to the floor laying rubber out across Old Highway 9 heading back toward Norman proper. BAM! BAM! he fired twice, blowing out both tires on the right-hand side of my parents' car. About a mile down the road one hubcap flew off. I pulled over soon where we changed the front tire. Then we hobbled into Norman and stopped at a phone booth where one of the Mikes called a friend who opened his gas station, came and got one of the tires and fixed it for us.

I got home just in time to face very angry parents waiting to take me to the downtown Oklahoma City recruiting station. I had to be there by six a.m., and there was barely enough time to get me there. What they had to say doesn't bear repeating, but when we walked back outside my father screamed WHERE THE HELL'S MY HUBCAP?

Boy was he pissed. So much so in fact that when we got to the recruiting station my dad was yelling; I couldn't get a word in edgewise; and Sergeant Johnson sized up the situation immediately. Come here, son, he said. You know, he lied, you've signed up for three years but if you'll go ahead and change your decision to four years you'll get more educational benefits on the GI Bill. (Eighteen months active duty bought all the GI Bill available.)

I reviewed the enlistment contract with curiosity. It seemed different somehow from the first time I'd gone over it. A blue logo, an eagle, stood spreadwinged above an asterisk-bordered name-and-address block in the upper left quadrant. Thirteen double-spaced one-liners ran the length of the page preceded by bullets along the margin.

Grinning Sergeant Johnson held out a red-inked, felt-tip pen. I took it, thinking this'll fix 'em – meaning my parents – and quickly ruled out one of the threes, then substituted a four beside it. Bright red ink bled into the white bond paper, coursing outward in vein-like rivulets. Quickly I initialed the change and moved to the next one, hurrying through each revision. A tingling ache enveloped my index finger preceding a numbing sensation. Ink sucked out the pen tip, it seemed, leaching through the spongy bond stationery.

Sergeant Johnson reached for the contract, then drew back suddenly as bright, early morning sunlight burst through an old stained glass window on the opposite side of the room. A shaft of intense reddish-white light shot toward us across the floor. It worked its way forward, up and over Sergeant Johnson's desk, high-lighted the blue eagle, then fired down the line of bullets and reflected straight into my eyes. I flinched, momentarily blinded, as Sergeant Johnson scooped up the contract with satisfaction written all over his face. You won't be sorry, he promised. Your country has asked and you have just given.

Sergeant (E-5) Johnson was Gunnery Sergeant (E-7) Johnson when I saw him nineteen months later, making both his promotions and money off the blood of ignorant, naive boys. I wished they'd sent his ass to our outfit where Sergeant Rotan would have seen clear through him to his gutless seams. He'd have come home in a body bag, or at least much more cognizant of his previously evil ways. You can bet your life on that. Nam had a way of changing assholes into angels and vice versa.

All for a lousy fifteen cents!

We were using up water fast. Guys were dropping all around us from heat exhaustion and respiratory problems. The razorblade-sharp elephant grass was as tall as the valley it grew in. Our point squad was hacking away, each man relieving another at regular intervals, the trailblazing with machetes kicking up enough dust to fill a grain bin. Sweat stung the scratches on our hands and arms, and attracted hungry swarming deerflies. The halizone-treated water tasted awful, like iodine, and it seemed dry. We soaked it up in the caked dust and pollen of our digestive tracts long before it found its way to our bladders. The Koolaid Kid was the first to pass out, followed immediately by two other heat casualties. Sugar rushed the water straight out his pores as quickly as he slurped it in.

A dust off chopper arrived from the south some twenty minutes later. Thropthropthropthropthrop it said as it hovered but couldn't land. I fell back hard against my pack exhausted and barely breathing. The wind farting outward from beneath the chopper blades felt good, real good, but smelled like fuel. I remember thinking My God, I can't move; I am totally wasted and something's seriously wrong. The temperature felt like 140 degrees. The humidity was unbelievable, drinkable even. Instinct warned me to break out a salt tablet, but I couldn't afford to waste the water necessary to get it down. Pollen and dust propped up by the fan blades mixed so thick we could barely breathe. Gnats swarming around my ears competed with the deerflies, diving and biting mercilessly. I couldn't even fight back. First squad had just loaded the third heat casualty when the big huey began to sink, drifting farther and farther away from me but closer and closer to the tops of the elephant grass. It struggled gently at first, trying to lift back up, and then more powerfully when all of a sudden FLASH, the whole area went up like a matchbox engulfing the chopper, back-blasting the grass below, fulminating skyward in a thick mushroom cloud of smoke.

I jerked to my feet and ran springing, crashing and hopping through tree-high grass. The fire was spreading fast. Everyone all around me was scrambling, stampeding. Many had abandoned their gear in the haste, not realizing just how stupid that really was until grenades and ammo started blowing up all over the place. Fire raged like a blast furnace.

I remember making it back to the tree line overlooking the valley before turning to see what was happening. The charred chopper upside down looked like a gigantic praying mantis. Fire spread out moving in a circle toward the trees. Smoke spiraled straight upward in humongous massive puffs. Six water-carrying dragon ships later came tearing out of the south, dropping thousands of gallons of putrid water on the whole area, rapidly turning the atmosphere from dust to smoke to stink.

An amazing thing was that no matter how tired we were, when the shit hit the fan our bodies responded with surges of powerful reserve energy. It felt something like catching your second wind, but ten times more potent.

The next morning Murphy moved toward the bushes that exploded. I could hear someone screaming in the distance, but when the sounds rapidly closed in and got louder I realized it was me and I got really scared. My whole body shook uncontrollably, and my head started banging against the ground.

You're okay, you're okay, soothed the Gunny, stroking my head and neck trying to comfort me while working on my wounds. You're a damn sight better off than the others over there, he said, pointing to where I'd been sitting, drinking coffee, just moments before.

Watson was moaning Momma, Momma, the terrible sounds rising in pitch and then reducing to groans and sobs. Murphy was everywhere to be found, and Stricklyn might as well have been dead, totally dead that is. Watson lived two and a half hours. Wiskey made it all the way to the next morning.

What happened? I whispered, wincing in pain, trying to sort it out in my head.

I heard it was all Murphy's fault, said Dave.

What happened? I repeated.

Jimmy told me Murphy taped the handle down on one of his grenades, he said. Supposedly he broke the pin on it last week.

Guess the tape rotted off.

I asked Jimmy about it later, and he said Watson told him. The official report read that he'd stepped on a mine in the bushes where he'd gone to take a whiz.

Stricklyn was there still, in the chopper on the floor at my feet. I couldn't look but then I couldn't not look either. We were in the air now, and fortunately my attention was eventually forced to the fire fight intensifying just north and below us. Air strikes had evidently been called. Boundary marking flares directed the attack of the two Phantom jet fighters that came roaring in out of nowhere, right behind their tracer rounds, strafing and restrafing the valley floor, then veering hard right before climbing upward, straight upward, noses damn near flipping backward, barely clearing the sheer-faced cliff wall of the mountain range beyond the valley.

On the third run, one pilot misjudged his timing, I guess, smashing and exploding into the cliff face. Huge columns of black smoke spiraled out and away from the wall, upward at first and then downward as pieces of the ship tumbled and crashed to the valley floor. There was a moment of silence then, everyone staring in shock as the second fighter tipped his wings twice before shooting into a climbing roll, a traditional farewell, ascending one final time out of the valley, then disappearing skyward in a bank of clouds, heading back to base.

I overviewed the once green but now black valley floor below, the smoke and fire, the scurrying troops, the enemy in flight moving rapidly before our advancing forces. I remember stealing one last peek at Stricklyn's pulsating body. Dark flies bombarded it from all directions, then lit for a second or two to feed on the blood before the gusting wind blew them off again. I felt cheated, robbed of an ideal. All my life I had been searching for the right to live life to the max, unshackled by social constraints, and now suddenly I realized that that meant chaos.

-10-

The Koolaid Kid was dead. We all had a hard time accepting that. Sikes was his real name. His mom sent him tons of Koolaid. He was thoroughly addicted to the stuff. He wouldn't drink water any other way. I couldn't blame him really.

Halizone-treated water sucks, said Surly. As long as you get it out of the five-gallon cans it's okay. As long as it comes from a lister bag it's okay too. But, he warned, when you fill your canteens from rivers or streams or creeks or lakes or rice paddies or bomb craters, then watch out cause one of two things will happen if you don't treat it with halizone tablets. Either you get the shits or you risk malaria. Almost all the water in Nam is disease ridden. The most disconcerting thing is filling your canteen not two feet away from Goddamn floating water-buffalo turds. Now get out there and fight the fuckers, he said, but don't drink their water.

Surly gave the same opening speech to every Newbie, every FNG. He was right about one thing though. Water buffalo turds were everywhere – probably because water buffalos were everywhere. A local's status could be measured by the size of his water buffalo herd. Many families owned at least one water buffalo. They treated their water buffalos better than they treated themselves. The water buffalo pens were better constructed than their own hooches. Kind of like the way many US farmers have better barns than homes. Water buffalos were extremely docile animals until they got around Americans. I don't know what it was about us, but we just seemed to bring out their skittish side.

I remember once during Operation Dewey Canyon down around Chu Lai when we accidentally walked up on one from behind. He reared up on his front legs and snap kicked backwards, smacking Joey in the chest so hard he flew back against a hooch porch support pole knocking it out from under the porch roof that came tumbling down on top of him and Jimmy.

God, everybody was bustin' guts, laughing hard when a single round from a .51 caliber machine gun suddenly opened up Roger's chest and then exited through a can of ham and lima beans in his backpack, splattering blood and soup all over my face and neck and down the front of my flak jacket.

Jesus, everybody went bananas at once. Raven blew away the water buffalo with the first bloop of his M-79. My immediate reaction was to blast away at the hooch in front of us, but my M-16 jammed after the first round. The M-16's buffer system left a lot to be desired. I threw the damned thing down in rage and was standing there weaponless when the .51 caliber opened up again, blasting chunks of flesh and bone out of the water buffalo's already dead carcass.

Momma San and Papa San frantically chattered at us from their squatting positions, waving fists in furious rage, gesturing back toward their dead pet water buffalo. Jimmy opened up on automatic scattering a neat pattern across Papa San's chest, neck and face blowing him off his feet and backward damn near through the straw-walled hooch. Momma San screamed, tears shooting out of her astonished face just as Joey blew her away like a kiss, creamed her like corn.

My God! My God! I thought as I worked my way toward Roger's body to get his M-16. The .51 caliber opened up again, this time shattering the thigh bone in Joey's right leg. He went down hard, splattering dirt with his sweat.

The Koolaid Kid was sitting on the fallen porch yelling I'M ALL OUTA FUCKIN' KOOLAID! He had his pack off and beside him, his canteen out and he was trying to mix Koolaid, all the time wiping at his eyes and nose with his sopping shirt sleeve. Tears flowed down his cheeks mixing with the snot running out of his nose onto his lips and into his mouth, his tongue flicking out as uncontrolled as everything else going down. I WANT MY KOOLAID! he kept screaming. I WANT MY KOOLAID!

Raven had his M-79 tucked up under his right arm like a shotgun. His .45 was in his left hand. He charged that .51 caliber nest Chesty Puller reincarnated, John Wayne himself, blooping and blasting and reloading one-handed like nobody and nothing I'd ever seen. His eyes were huge and bulging out like they'd pop any second, his mouth spread tight and wide, his teeth bared, his throat growling and gurgling and spitting and all the time alternately firing the .45 and the M-79.

I laid there writhing in the dirt praying the Lord's Prayer mixing it up with the Act of Contrition and the Hail Mary, yelling GOD GET ME OUTA HERE, the rank stench of spoiling ham and lima beans and old blood rising up through my quivering snorting nostrils. The .51 caliber was gone by the time Raven got to the gun site. The Koolaid Kid was a basket case. And I was stalking his shadow, now, while getting still shorter – only FIFTY DAYS until my drop dead date.

-11-

Who hasn't gone on R&R? asked the Gunny.

I haven't, I lied, raising my hand and waving it frantically like Marty sitting beside me. I had FORTY DAYS to go. Nobody in the company was as short as I was; nobody was even close, except Raven and Malcolm.

The Gunny looked surprised at first, wondering how come I hadn't gone yet. You wanna go to Phnom Penh, Rootie? he asked.

Sure, Gunny! I said, knowing that as soon as I got to Da Nang where all I-Corps R&R flights departed I could finagle my way back to Bangkok. Lucky for me the Gunny didn't check personnel records until after I'd gone. He was furious when I got back, but he understood. Skating as much as possible was a way of life in Nam. Literally.

In Bangkok I teamed up with Iggy and Kaiko again. They were as happy to see me as I them. My first demand was a Turkish bath. It took three baths before the water turned grey instead of black, five before I finally felt as though I wasn't wallowing in my own filth.

You bookoo dirty, bookoo dirty, Kaiko kept saying, shaking her head side to side as she scrubbed and rubbed and scrubbed some more.

You have to realize we go anywhere from a couple of days to a couple of months without being able to bathe, I told her.

I was already blitzed pretty much to the max by the time Iggy, Kaiko and I began bar-hopping our way toward further oblivion. I was worried about Marty back in the hotel room. He had gotten sick two nights earlier, his teeth chattering so bad I thought they'd break, but then that stopped and he was okay until later when his fever rose with the sweat pouring out his skin. God he was hot but he wouldn't let me call a doctor. And then he seemed all right again until we got on the plane where he barfed all over the men's room. He was still sweating bad when we got off the plane. By the time we checked into the hotel and made it to our rooms, he was so much worse I made him hit the sack. Sweat was pouring off his face soaking the bed sheets beneath him.

Go on, he said, I'll be okay. I ain't dying till I strike it rich.

So I went on, telling him I'd check up on him as soon as I got back.

A band was playing Righteous Brothers music when I stumbled on stage, grabbed the mic, and bellowed *Unchained Melody* as best I could, totally out of sync, the lead singer laughing and shouting the words in my ear, the whole place cracking up, flashbulbs flashing, Iggy and Kaiko trying desperately to drag me back down off stage.

By the time we got back to the hotel, Marty needed a doctor bad. His pulse was sky high and he couldn't hardly breathe or talk when he whispered I...can't make it, Rootie. I'm...gonna die.

I screamed at Iggy to go get the doctor who called me aside to say, He's got malaria, son, complicated by pneumonia; he won't make it till daylight. I've done all I can. He's got Plasmodium falciparum.

No, Doc, you can't be serious, I said. He was fine until a couple of days before we got on the plane.

I'm sorry, said the doctor.

Rootie? called Marty weakly. Call my mom...Rootie. Tell her...I wanna come home.

I ran down the stairs all confused looking for a telephone booth but couldn't find one. A clerk asked if I needed help and I said Yes, that's exactly what I need. I sat down on the stairs trying to calm myself thinking, Okay it's the dope, it's all a dream, I'll come down and everything'll be okay.

But when I came down Marty came down too, on a stretcher, with a blanket over his face, and his arm hanging out to one side, lifelessly flopping up and down keeping beat to the unsynchronized steps of his four stretcher bearers, and Kaiko's soft background wailing.

-12-

GAS! GAS! someone shouted, and I thought My god I didn't bring my mask. THIRTY DAYS to go and I'm gonna die. I tore my first aid kit open, nervously digging out the atropine unit, shakily preparing for self injection. I had been holding my breath for a minute or so when someone yelled It's only tear gas.

I remember coughing and crying for several minutes, thankful it wasn't organophosphate. The stories we'd been told in bootcamp were excessively nerve wracking. Although tear gas was painful, at least we could survive it. In this particular instance what had happened was our own men had discovered a gook stronghold, into which they had fired several tear gas canisters. Being downwind, my unit suffered the side-effects. Six gooks were captured though and turned over to the local ARVNs in Phu Bai. The next day six new bodies joined those on Suicide Row.

Suicide Row was about twenty-five yards of taut barbed wire fence line just outside the Phu Bai military compound on the south side. Naked corpses of spies and prisoners were hung or otherwise stranded there. Their contorted, knotted up, surgically deformed and otherwise violated bodies stood as deterrents against future membership in Communist networks. It was jokingly called Suicide Row.

ARVNs had very little patience. I believe that many of the atrocities attributed to American military forces were in fact committed by the Army of the Republic of South Vietnam. ARVNs also had very little to do in Nam's I-Corps area in comparison with US forces.

Oh sure, said Rotan one day, they guard the bridges along Highway 1, but then the bridges get blown up as fast as they're built or rebuilt. Sure looks like inside jobs from here.

-13-

I lucked out and contracted immersion foot for the second time when I was down to only TWENTY DAYS. Immersion foot is a crippling ailment that results from getting sand in your soaking wet

173

boots. The sand quickly chafes away at your dish-water soft feet until they crack, get a fungus infection and then turn raw and bloody. It usually isn't long before you can't even put socks on let alone walk. Immersion foot stopped whole company operations more effectively than gook snipers or mortar attacks.

Five days in the rear, said the Corpsman.

Anything you say, Doc, I replied.

-14-

At TEN DAYS I made the mistake of losing all my money in an acey-deucy game. Acey-deucy is one of those fun games that'll make or break you. Military Payment Currency or MPC looked just like Monopoly money. Because of that, I think, it had less value. Losing $100 in MPC had less psychological effect than losing $10 in greenbacks. MPC looked so much like play money we just wasted it every time we turned around. Anyway, I was holding the King of Clubs and the Two of Diamonds so I bet my last $300 thinking that, short as I was, I couldn't lose. I drew the Ace of Spades and couldn't sleep for three days, convinced it had to be an omen.

-15-

HOMEWARD BOUND!
I wish I was.
Home, where my thought's escape me.
Home, where my music's playing.
Home, where my loved life's waiting silently for me.

My Freedom Flight was scheduled to leave Da Nang airport November 8, 1967, in just FIVE MORE DAYS at two in the afternoon. There would be a two-day layover in Okinawa before departure for the real world. God I'm gettin' short, I thought.

- I am knee high to a grasshopper.
- Need a ladder to climb stairs.
- Can throw a shot-put from under a parked car.
- Can walk upright under a snake's belly.
- Can't see over my hardon when I wake in the morning.
- Can sleep sittin' up under a rock.
- Can drown myself in a thimble.
- Have to piss up in the air to fill a urine sample.
- Have to reach up to wipe a worm's butt.
- Have to look up to find down.

God I'm so short got to jump up to kiss an ant's ass.

-16-

We were high above the clouds, but descending. The setting moon was big and full and seemed to be moving closer and closer. I knew I was imagining it, was positive in fact, and yet there was Benjie, right in the middle of the moon, big as life and laughing, laughing like he didn't have a care in the world. I tried to snap out of it, fight the tears, look away. God, it was confusing.

Matt was really special, I remember thinking, chosen perhaps. Like that time in church just before he died, when he was performing one of his altar boy functions and I was sitting in one of the pews between his mom and younger brother Gary. His dad and older brother Mike were there too. There were twelve couples walking down the aisle, the boys each carrying a rose. Matt and his partner brought up the rear. They were filing up to the statue of the Blessed Virgin Mary and genuflecting just before placing the roses in the vase at her foot.

Afterwards, about halfway home (Matt and I and his parents were in one car, Michael and Gary and a couple of neighbor girls in another) Matt's mom asked whether anyone had noticed anything strange during Mass. When nobody said anything she just ups and blurts out: I know it can't be but when Matthew placed his rose in the vase, Mother Mary looked down at him and smiled.

I tell you it got real quiet in the car. The words had rushed out of

175

her mouth, and she just sat there with her head down and her hands folded. I suppose I just imagined it, she sighed. I glanced over at Matt and he scrunched up his nose the way he did sometimes whenever he was trying to look innocent, his red bangs swept down across his forehead shielding the gleam in both blue eyes.

Then, a couple of hours later, when we were all seated around the dinner table passing food and everything, little Gary butts in and asks if anyone besides him noticed the Virgin Mary looking down and smiling at Matthew that morning. Man, everything just plain stopped, except for Matt's mom who fainted out of her chair. It was weird. Everyone jumped up to help. Her eyes rolled back and her legs were flopping. I didn't know what to do.

A couple of months later I went over to visit Mr. and Mrs. Slade, Matt's parents. The house was all shut up, and it was August. Matt's mom and dad both opened the door.

Hello Terry, they said. Come in and have a seat. How are you?

Not so good, I answered. I miss Matt.

We miss him too, said Mrs. Slade, but he's okay now. He's happy.

He came by to visit the other night, said Mr. Slade.

We were sound asleep, interrupted Mrs. Slade, when suddenly I just woke up. I mean popped right up in bed. I turned toward the window, which was open you know. We always leave it open this time of year. Oh, she exclaimed, the moon was so full, so beautiful, and the curtains were blowing ever so gently, and the light was so bright, so intense. I just sat there staring at it, and it started moving toward the window, getting closer and bigger, and I got a little nervous and started thumping on Hank here, on his arm.

Yeah, said Mr. Slade. I woke up wondering what the heck I'd done 'cause she'd never hit on me in my sleep before, leastwise I don't think so, and then I noticed this here light so I rolled over.

And the moon, butt in Mrs. Slade again, the moon just floated in through that window like it was a big door and moved across the room, and then it just hovered there at the foot of the bed and the whole room was bathed in bright, warm, glowing light.

Uh huh, agreed Mr. Slade shaking his head up and down, and then suddenly, suddenly that moon was Matthew.

Yes! said Mrs. Slade emphatically. That moon turned into my Matthew's face and he was smiling and all happy-looking just like when he was a little boy and I used to rock him in my lap. And you know what he said? He said Don't worry about me Momma. I'm doing fine where I am. It's wonderful here and I'm happy, so don't worry anymore. And then his face faded and the moon backed away toward the window and floated back outside again and into the sky.

Mr. Slade rose up out of his seat shaking his head, his eyes all trance-like as he turned and left the room. I stood to leave too.

Matthew was special, said Mrs. Slade. Her eyes were all watery and her lips trembled.

I know, I told her. All the kids thought so. I'll always remember him, Mrs. Slade. He was a brother to me.

She reached out and touched me, and then walked off toward where her husband had gone.

I found my own way to the door.

-17-

Sir, are you all right? You've been staring for hours. Are you okay sir? We're nearly ready to land. Please fasten your seatbelt.

I could hear her voice, but it seemed to be coming from so far away. I think I nodded. Fuck the seatbelt, I wanted to say.

-18-

Son, you're very lucky, said the doctor. None of the thirteen pieces of shrapnel in you has done any really serious damage. There's one in your back I'm going to leave there though. It's too deep to dig out. I'd just make a bigger unnecessary scar there. It's not close to anything vital so you shouldn't have any complications later. In fact, it's quite possible it'll work itself out. Same thing with this one in your left hand here, he said, pointing to the back of my left middle finger near the center knuckle. It's too near the surface to bother messing with. It'll for sure work itself out someday.

You're real lucky with the one in your leg, too. Another half inch and it would have severed the artery. In fact, I'd say this book saved your life, he said, holding the inch thick book I'd been carrying in my left jungle-utility leg pocket. It was a copy of *The Devil's Advocate* or *The Devil's Own Advocate* (I can't remember the title) by Taylor Caldwell or Caldwell Taylor (I can't keep that straight either). I do remember that it was an excellent book and I was enjoying it a lot and I was nearly through reading it. It had something to do with America becoming a police state. The piece of shrapnel that hit my leg went through the book first. That slowed it down just enough to prevent its hitting my artery. Those two pieces of shrapnel never did work their way out. One's a curiosity that turns up every time my back is x-rayed, and the other's a conversation piece people notice looks like a mole. They are a nuisance because they ache every time it rains or the weather turns cold.

-19-

I looked out the window through the fog, then tried to focus on my blurred reflection in the glass. Twenty-five minutes later we broke beneath the clouds pointed toward El Toro airfield and landed on the rain soaked runway. It wasn't quite light yet. A very fine mist wrung steadily from above. God I hate rain, I thought. It's so hard to see clearly when it's raining. And the whole world seems like it's crying. Not a sound from anyone. The Freedom Bird was totally quiet. How very, very strange. Three hundred and ninety some days we had waited for this, the year of fear behind us, the moment we'd all lived for here at last, the moment we'd all dreamed of now a reality. I twisted around to face two hundred or so vacant-eyed, expressionless mirror images. The thousand yard stare we called it.

FREE-DUMB! yelled someone suddenly like a sonic boom.

YEAH! I thought. Life's a bitch – but I didn't die. Wish you were here:

Stricklyn, and
JB, and
Kody, and
Wiskey, and
Marty, and
Bendix, and
Tommy, and
Roger, and
Carl, and
Money, and
Seldom, and
Bostick, and
Morgan, and
John, and
Jake, and
Rotan, and
Mac, and
McKlusky, and
Wagner, and
Frank, and
David, and
Hoover, and
Beardly, and
Joey, and
Bursar, and
Pete, and
C-More, and
Nebraska, and
Watson, and
Marvin, and
Dixon, and
Jerome, and
Walker, and
Chris, and
Malcolm, and
Little, and
Les, and

Smoke, and
George, and
Gunny, and
Birch, and
Rock, and
Raven, and
Jimmy, and
Lugar, and
Dave, and
Surly, and
Kelsey, and
Walter, and
Sparky, and
Ricky, and
Travis, and
Shorty, and
Murphy, and
Sikes, and
Benjie, and Benjie, and Benjie.

EPILOGUE

Terry P. Rizzuti

EPILOGUE

Many years have passed. Those closest call me Terry now, but I still think of myself as Rootie, a kid that learned life's unfair, has no balance, and had that concept slapped upside his head time and again. What I've learned as Terry, however, is an understanding that we create our own destiny. I've come to that late, having just turned 64, and now very much believe in the notion that some of us become destined, i.e., obligated and to a certain extent even honored, to identify our life's purpose, plus work to achieve that purpose to the best of our abilities. My destiny was to survive the Vietnam War, educate myself well enough to write about it, and pass that knowledge to others. That's it in a nutshell. That I believe in my destiny might suggest to some that I also believe in a personal God that takes care of me. I wouldn't go that far, but I certainly believe in an afterlife.

I could feel the light. It's so difficult to sleep once I sense light. I sat up, swung one leg off the side of the bed, reached for the cord and pulled open the window shade. It was raining, but not hard. There beyond the cloud line in the southwest, I could see the truly full Blue Moon moving in the wrong direction, backwards toward our window, slowly at first, and then more quickly. I looked over my shoulder at Mary, my wife. She was sound asleep, snoring raspidly. I love that about her, that she can sleep, and through nearly anything.

I looked back at the moon and she was framed in its glow – that little girl again. She slid through the window quickly to the foot of the bed, then hovered there. They don't surprise me anymore, her visits; she comes in dreams so vivid they are real. You'd think that an old man could get past his 45-year-old war, but not me. That war, that damned Vietnam War consumes me still, defines who I am and dictates my daily routine.

They're always the same, her visits – sudden – but I welcome them now. She looks like I feel – tired. I was hoping it was Matt or Benjie this time, I tell her.

You don't owe them what you owe me.

I start to argue, but instead ask What is it you want?

I want the last word, she says.

What do you mean?

It's my story, she says.

No it's not, I say, I wrote it. Besides, it's already been published.

Where do you think the words come from? she asks.

From me, from my heart. I tap on my chest.

No, she says, they come from me, my soul. She spreads her arms, palms forward, then continues. Before we met, all you could muster was gibberish. Parts 2 and 3 would have been as unreadable as the first draft of Part 1 was. I'm the one that helped you make sense of it all, and I'm the one that brought you the letters.

I thought back to the last day of July, 1985, the day Me's letters arrived. She had called to see if I was attending our 20th high school reunion. I told her no, that I was busy writing a book about my war experiences. I've got your old letters, she said, the ones you wrote me from Vietnam. You're kidding, I said. Do you want them? she asked. An uneasy feeling took hold, a shiver that skittered through my bones. Let me think about it, I said, and we left it at that, until sometime later when I called and asked her to send them.

And then life intervened and I forgot about the letters. But one day as I strolled home from work, I came to the corner near my house and stopped to look for traffic. There, kitty-corner, stood a two- or three-year-old little girl in a bright red pajama blouse. She was staring at me and looked angry. My first thought was who is this little girl; why is she alone? But then suddenly my heart raced and sweat rushed to my skin. I looked in the other direction toward my house. A big manila envelope was sticking out of the mailbox, and my second thought was The letters, the letters! Quickly I looked back toward the little girl but she was gone, just like that, a figment maybe.

Oh god no, I thought, and raced across the street. I grabbed the letters from the box and rushed into the house. Please god no, I said, and tore into the envelop. Please god no repeated like a machine gun as I sorted through them. No, no, no, I prayed, quickly scanning though April and May 1967 until I found it – The Letter – the one dated May 24th, the letter that drove home to me exactly who I was and what I am – a murderer. I started shaking, crying on the couch, soaking my beard. I cried until my tear ducts ran dry, then walked outside to see if I could find her, to tell her I was sorry. That's something I do often – look for her to tell her I'm sorry – but I never find her, even though, like now, she often finds me. And like I said, I welcome her visits now. At least she no longer looks angry, so I keep hoping that before I die she'll smile. I'm not counting on it, because I sure wouldn't smile if someone destroyed my home, my family, my life

What do you mean *you* brought the letters? I ask.

Who do you think saw to it that Me saved them, and then sent them to you? She didn't want to, you know, send them that is. Those letters were the only love you ever gave her. She didn't want to turn loose of them.

You assign yourself too much credit. Me made her own choices.

I want the last word, she demanded again, adamantly.

I'm not convinced you deserve the last word. *The Second Tour* isn't your story, it's mine. I slaved over it for years, lost sleep, discarded marriage, suffered through dozens of rejections from publishers, even watched more wars unfold and replace mine.

Who do you think woke you at night to work on it?

Your mother did, I said, always trying to stab me with that damn knife. I nearly had a heart attack every time she came at me.

That's right, but who do you think sent her, and why? All your life you've only responded from fear. That's why your father beat you, that's why your mother slapped you up-side your hard-head, that's why your classmates beat on you when you wouldn't keep your mouth shut. I sent Mother after you because it worked; it got you out of feeling sorry for yourself and into writing. She enjoyed it of course, immensely in fact. You're lucky I didn't send Father. He'd have killed you. He tried to, twice. Remember when you and Top Sergeant Turvey had that wreck? If you hadn't been so drunk, you'd be dead. And remember that wreck in Oklahoma City? That was Father who stomped on that guy's accelerator and crashed his truck into your car door. I don't know how you survived that one.

I think you're making this all up just to get what you want, I said.

And who do you think saw to it that you found your way into English classes and learned a little about literature? And who made sure you went to graduate school so you'd meet Jin?

Don't make me laugh, I said; there's no way you have that much control.

Somebody had to introduce you to Faulkner, help you understand the power of style and voice. Somebody had to make sure you learned that jocks shouldn't feel embarrassed just because they have brains. Jin did that for you. Besides, you needed his friendship. Thirty-something years old and you didn't have a single friend. How pitiful was that?

You think you have all the answers, don't you?

We could have taken your daughter like Father wanted to. Poetic justice, he argued, and he was right, but I talked him out of it. I didn't want *us* to become *you*.

I was starting to get angry. I could feel my face stretch. It has always been that way with me – in place of enlightenment, I find anger instead.

And who do you think brought Wil into your life? Do you think that was an accident? Do you think it was some grand coincidence that led him from The University of Oklahoma to the Air Force Academy where he'd one day teach *The Second Tour* to some of your country's future military leaders?

I didn't know what to say.

And who connected you with Professor Don so you'd be published in *War, Literature and the Arts*? Was that a coincidence, too? And didn't that connect you with Drs. Tom, Dan and Nathan at Regis University? Were those mere coaccidentals, as you're fond of saying? Hasn't your life improved for having met those people? Haven't they taught you *anything*? Haven't you *learned* from having interacted with them and their students?

She's right, I thought, my life has been bettered by all she says, but I'm not convinced she's the reason I've told this story, although others certainly think so. Wil teaches her story in behavioral sciences classes. Dan, Tom and Nathan teach it through the *Center for the Study of War Experience*. It's just a question of time before she's immortalized in literature.

And they, the professors, they ask me to speak, make public appearances at conferences and seminars, explain what I did and why. Sometimes I refuse because it's not easily put into context, not by any stretch, but it's important to try. People need to know that bad things happen to good people in war zones, that the horror of war is the resultant "collateral damage."

But I talk about other things, too. I talk about the therapeutic value of art, how things like writing or painting or music can serve as self-therapy. And I talk about how proud I am to have been a combat Marine that survived conditions that would kill most Americans in a mere few days or weeks. I talk about how memory can't be trusted, especially war memory, which comes through a biased and often damaged perspective. And I talk about war literature, how it's born under fire and teaches us more about the human condition than any other source, giving us our villains, true, but also our heroes, so I talk about my personal heroes, the ones who didn't make it home. In many ways, they're just like that little girl, ghosts that reach out, shouting at me to tell their stories. So I do, because when I see them again, I want them to know I did my best, my damnedest to show their lives had meaning.

Look, I said, you make it sound like I shouldn't get any credit, like I've just been your conduit all these years. You're saying everything is predetermined for us. I used to believe that, but I'm not so certain anymore.

Not everything is predetermined, she said, not for everyone, but the second you pulled that trigger you forfeited the right to call your life your own, activated the curse of reliving your past. And the second you decided to atone, you welded your life to mine. Because of that, that's mostly what you have been – a conduit. I'm the one that brought you Mary, for example, when you needed calmness, spiritual grounding and love. You needed to be loved and taught to love. *I gave you that through her.* And I brought you Dr. Louis when you needed confirmation that *The Second Tour* was worth the paper it was printed on, and Dr. Peter at the University of Kentucky, and your buddy Ray when you needed another friend, someone to help convince you to seek psychiatric counseling, plus help you find a way out of writer's block.

I looked at her, hard and long. She was starting to fade. The moon rose from the bed and was beginning to recede back out the window. The rain had stopped. Who are you? I called out to her, are you God?

You're such a Jarhead, she sneered. No I'm not God, and He isn't *boys* either. I'm just that little girl. After all that education, all this time, are you still so dense I have to spell this out for you?

Yes, I said; I learn from directness, remember? from a slap upside the head.

She rolled her eyes. "I don't know how to make it any clearer, Terry. It's all about fairness, about balance – you took my life; I gave you yours."

Terry P. Rizzuti

READER'S GUIDE

Terry P. Rizzuti

READER'S GUIDE

This guide takes the form of questions appropriate for the reader to ask of *The Second Tour*. It is not intended to be exhaustive, nor is it necessary to address every question in order to enjoy or understand *The Second Tour*.

Writers of literature think of fiction as their canvas, their workspace for developing ideas. Fiction is therefore a created world within which each word and idea has been chosen. The product thus developed, whether it be a novel, short story or whatever, is a world mediated by a series of choices made by the author.

To understand the intent of a work, the reader must become aware of the choices made by the author, and the pattern of those choices. As the writer develops ideas, he or she also develops the various elements of fiction. The questions that follow are intended to draw attention to *The Second Tour's* fictive elements in a way that makes evident the reasons Rizzuti chose them.

Point of view (POV) is a story's angle of narration. In *The Second Tour*, the reader encounters the first-person POV, as narrated through Rootie, the main character.

1: What advantage does this first-person POV give the author?

2: Is Rootie trustworthy? To answer this question, ask yourself: is Rootie "normal"? is Rootie in a position to give the reader a particular insight, for example the bird's-eye view as opposed to the worm's-eye view? Also ask yourself, does Rootie's position change significantly during the novel?

Characterization is a term used to describe the author's created characters within the fictive world. What and how the reader learns about each character is important to a full understanding of each character. For example, the reader can learn about a character from the narrator, or from the character's own actions or words, or through the actions or words of other characters.

1: What and how does the reader learn about Rootie?

2: What and how does the reader learn about C-More, Benjie, Rotan, Malcolm and Raven?

3: What are the interrelationships among the six characters in 1 & 2 above, and what significance do the interrelationships have?

4: What role does Rootie's high school friend, Matt, play?

5: Are you involved with the characters? (i.e., approving, disapproving, empathizing, sympathizing, dispassionate, etc.) If so, why?

Tone is a quality of the work as a whole that contributes to the development in the reader of an attitude desired by the author. It should never be confused with the author's attitude.

1: What is the tone (mood) of *The Second Tour*?

2: How does the author develop this tone?

3: Is the tone consistent throughout the work? If not, where do the shifts in tone occur, and what do the shifts provide for the work?

Structure

1: Describe the character conflicts in the work and whether they are character-against-character conflicts, or character-against-self. Use Rootie, Rotan and Malcolm to answer.

2: What is the basis for the conflicts? (physical? intellectual? moral? emotional? natural?)

3: Action in *The Second Tour* is not linear-sequential (i.e., each incident logically following the previous). What does this choice accomplish?

4: What purposes do the following divisions serve in *The Second Tour*?
   a: Part 1?
   b: Part 2?
   c: Part 3, including the list of names at the end?
   d: The Prologue? The Epilogue?

5: How do the letters function in *The Second Tour*?
   a: Why does the author include the letters?
   b: Why does Rootie write the letters? What overall purpose do they serve him?
   c: Do the letters assist in revealing Rootie's character development? How?
   d: Do the letters assist in revealing changes that have occurred "back home."
   e: What is the relationship between the first and last letter?

6: What function do the marriage scenes serve, and why are the scenes broken up instead of physically connected?

7: What is the meaning of the title *The Second Tour*.

Theme is the statement that the total work makes about itself. Its concern is the work as a whole, its meaning. Theme is NOT: How does it turn out! Theme is NOT: What happens!

1: What is the central theme of *The Second Tour*?
   a: Is it Physical (emphasis on forces of nature)?
   b: Is it Emotional (man/woman seen in light of individual needs)?
   c: Is it Social (man/woman seen in context of social reality)?
   d: Is it Metaphysical (man/woman seen as spiritual entity)?

2: What does *The Second Tour* teach us about:
   a: War? The Vietnam War?
   b: The military? The Marine Corps?
   c: Officers vs. Enlisted Men?
   d: Social change?
   e: Boys vs. Manhood?
   f: Post Traumatic Stress Disorder (PTSD?
      i: Loss of life on one's psyche?
      ii: Loss of friendships?
      iii: Loss of spiritual self (one's moral compass)?
      iv: Support for the troops?

3: What role does the leech play as metaphor?

4: What is the meaning of the phrase "God is boys," and what is its effect on Rootie?

5: Discuss the meaning of the following quote from Chapter 11 in terms of the letter found in Chapter 33: "On another level I believe stopping it means exposing the horror until the horror is conscious to everyone. Kind of like attacking the problem through the back door."

ABOUT THE AUTHOR

Terry P. Rizzuti was born in Stillwater, Oklahoma, in 1946, the son of first-generation Italian-Americans. He spent much of his early youth in Rome, New York, and surrounding towns before moving back to Oklahoma in 1965. He joined the Marine Corps in 1966 and served a tour in the northern I-Corps area of South Vietnam as a "grunt" from October 1966 to November 1967 assigned to the 2nd Squad, 2nd Platoon of Golf Company, 2nd Battalion, 26th Marine Regiment, alternately attached to the 1st and 3rd Marine Divisions. He was awarded the Purple Heart for shrapnel wounds received on May 2, 1967.

Rizzuti graduated with an English Literature degree from the University of Oklahoma (OU) in 1977, and then completed two years of graduate-level literature studies. He worked in various OU positions between 1980 and 1996, and helped found OU's Vietnam Memorial Scholarship Association. He is a life member of The American Legion, The Veterans of Foreign Wars, The Disabled American Veterans, and The Khe Sanh Veterans Association.

Currently, Rizzuti is a writer living in Estes Park, Colorado. *The Second Tour*, his first novel, was begun in 1984.

Lightning Source UK Ltd.
Milton Keynes UK
UKOW051228020212

186529UK00002B/22/P